WALKS & TOURS SICILY

YOUR TAILOR-MADE TRI STARTS HERE

Tailor-made trips and unique adventures crafted by local experts

Rough Guides has been inspiring travellers with lively and thought-provoking guidebooks for more than 35 years. Now we're linking you up with selected local experts to craft your dream trip. They will put together your perfect itinerary and book it at local rates.

Don't follow the crowd – find your own path.

HOW ROUGHGUIDES.COM/TRIPS WORKS

STEP 1

Pick your dream destination, tell us what you want and submit an enquiry.

STEP 2

Fill in a short form to tell your local expert about your dream trip and preferences.

STEP 3

Our local expert will craft your tailor-made itinerary. You'll be able to tweak and refine it until you're completely satisfied.

STEP 4

Book online with ease, pack your bags and enjoy the trip! Our local expert will be on hand 24/7 while you're on the road.

CONTENTS

Introduction

Trip plans

Directory

Baroque at its best

Succumb to Sicilian Baroque in Noto, Ragusa and Scicli in the Val di Noto Unesco World Heritage site (tour 10), and see splendid restored Baroque churches and palaces in Ortigia, Siracusa's island centre (walk 9).

Best walks & tours for...

Castles

Sweep away the cobwebs by visiting great medieval castles, including those in Erice (walk 5), Enna (walk 8), Siracusa (walk 9) and Catania (walk 11), built by the Normans or Swabians.

Island hoppers

Sail on ferries or hydrofoils to the stunningly beautiful Aeolian Islands (tour 14) off the northeast coast, popular for volcano-climbing and viewing, wallowing in mud baths, hiking, sailing and swimming.

Markets

The teeming markets of Palermo (walk 1) and Catania (walk 11), with mountains of glistening fresh produce and raucous street life, are riveting spectacles. Dive in early to see them at their best.

Mosaic art

Admire the Byzantine Norman mosaics in Palermo's Cappella Palatina (walk 1), the cathedrals of Cefalù (walk 3) and Monreale (tour 4), then visit Villa Romana del Casale (walk 8) for superb Roman floor mosaics.

Top museums

Discover outstanding collections of prehistoric and classical archaeological remains in the museums of Agrigento (walk 7), Siracusa (walk 9), Palermo (walk 1) and Lípari (tour 14).

Top temples

Sicily has more ancient Greek temples than Greece. Track down the most splendid at Agrigento (walk 7), Segesta (tour 4) and Selinunte (tour 6), and in summer stay for Greek drama under the stars in Siracusa's Teatro Greco.

Volcanoes and views

Explore Sicily's dramatically active volcanoes: a cable car, trail-bashing jeep tour or climb up Etna (tour 13), a hike up smouldering Vulcano or a view of the exploding cone of Strómboli from the sea (tour 14).

INTRODUCTION

An introduction to Sicily and what makes it special, what not to miss and what to do when you're there.

Discover Sicily

Goethe found Sicily intoxicating, from the Classical temples and Etna's eruptions to the volcanic Sicilians themselves. 'To have seen Italy without seeing Sicily', he wrote, 'is not to have seen Italy at all – for Sicily is the key to everything.'

Sicily's strategic maritime setting, at the crossroads of Mediterranean trade routes, has always played a crucial role in the island's history. Phoenicians, Greeks, Carthaginians, Romans, Arabs, Normans and Spaniards all left their mark, embellishing the island with some of their finest works and creating a beguiling cultural hybrid.

The varied legacies are redolent in the complex traditions and customs, as well as the diversity of architectural styles. It's perhaps not surprising that Sicilians see themselves as a separate nation from mainland Italy or the rest of Europe. When they cross the 4km (2.5-mile) Strait of Messina to the Italian peninsula, they're off to *'il Continente'*.

Many islanders still speak the Sicilian dialect, a rich Romance language sprinkled with words from Latin, Greek, Arabic, French and Spanish. The food – one of the great pleasures of a visit to Sicily – is different too, drawing from the culinary culture of Arabs and other invaders.

Sicily's fascination lies in the unexpected. Mount Etna's smoking plumes hover above scented citrus groves, Greek temple columns support a Baroque cathedral, exotic Arab-Norman churches glow with Byzantine mosaics, city street markets are tinged with the flavour of a Moroccan souk. Sicilian experiences know no bounds. You can ski in the morning, sunbathe in the afternoon, gaze into a bubbling volcanic crater one day, bathe from volcanic rocks the next. Another day you could marvel at mosaics in a Roman emperor's hunting villa, visit a valley of Greek temples or watch a Greek drama unfold in an ancient theatre under the stars.

Geography and layout

Lying halfway between Gibraltar and the Suez Canal, Sicily is the largest island in the Mediterranean and Italy's largest region. At 25,708 sq km (9,926 square miles) it is far bigger than most first-time visitors imagine, and while motorways help cut journey times, much of the island is mountainous and slow going. For example, crossing the island from Trápani in the west to Siracusa in the east takes at least

Sicilian local

four hours even by motorway. The landscape, whose diversity is unmatched by other Mediterranean islands, is one of mountains, citrus groves, pastureland and vast expanses of rolling wheatfields. The scenery is monumentally dramatic around Mount Etna, which dominates, and periodically threatens, the eastern coast. But Sicily is not all scenic. Around many of the cities there are great swathes of unsightly development, much of it modern unregulated blocks built by the Mafia. While some historic sites stand in blissful isolation, others, such as the glorious Greek relics in Agrigento's Valley of the Temples, are encroached upon by the modern world.

To cover the main cities and sights in one trip you'll need a good fortnight and at least two bases. If touring, you'd ideally fly into Palermo or Trápani in the west and out of Catania in the east. The itineraries in the book begin with Palermo (and Cefalù in Palermo province), then move around the coastline in a westerly direction.

The west coast is followed by a tour of the famous temples of Agrigento and an inland foray to hilltop Enna and the Roman Villa at Piazza Armerina. On the east coast, walks are devoted to each of Siracusa, Catania and the popular resort of Taormina, with inland tours of the Baroque gems of the southeast and the foothills of dominant Mount Etna. Last come the glorious Aeolian Islands, which float off the Tyrrhenian coast. All around the island you will see the Trinacria, the ancient symbol of Sicily, which became the official public flag in 2000. It features the head of Medusa with three wheat ears (symbolising the fertile land) and three bent legs (representing the island's three points).

Climate and when to visit

Sicily enjoys a mild Mediterranean climate, with hot, dry summers. The only extremes you can expect are in July and August, when daytime temperatures average 28°C (82°F) with highs slipping into the 40s at times. During this period it can be unbearably hot and crowded, especially in August when Italians take their summer holidays. Those choosing to visit in the height of summer should be prepared to spend the hottest hours indoors or under a parasol. It is always a good idea to take along a pair of sturdy, closed shoes if you are planning to hike. Generally, the best times to go are April, when spring flowers carpet the hillsides, through to mid-June, then from September to October/November. During these periods it's cooler and less crowded, and the sea is often still warm in November. Winters along the coast are short and generally mild, though many resort hotels and restaurants are closed. In the interior, especially the mountainous areas, temperatures

Tango dancers in Palermo

Fish market in Catania

are lower and Mount Etna remains snowcapped until late April or May, often offering marvellous eruptions with lava melting the snow. The Aeolian Islands are subject to strong winds and the main season is relatively short – from June to September.

The Sicilians

Islanders see themselves as Sicilian first and Italian second. In his masterpiece *The Leopard*, Giuseppe Tomasi di Lampedusa described them as follows: 'Sicilians never wish to improve for the simple reason that they believe themselves perfect. Their vanity is stronger than their misery. Every invasion by outsiders upsets their illusion of achieved perfection, and risks disturbing their self-satisfied waiting for nothing at all'. Although they have a reputation for being brooding, suspicious and inscrutable, closer contact reveals stoicism, conservatism and deep sensibility. This contradictory character doesn't match the sunny Mediterranean stereotype of *dolce far niente*, but visitors may nonetheless encounter overwhelming hospitality. Whether you're staying in the simplest *agriturismo* (farm-stay), a sumptuous palace with a Baroque ballroom or a boutique wine resort, the generous Sicilian spirit remains the same. The islanders are welcoming to visitors and love any occasion to socialise generally, whether it is at one of the street markets or one of the many festivals that all towns and cities celebrate at some time during the year. Food, and the pleasure of eating together, are considered one of the most important aspects of life. If you happen to be invited to a Sicilian home, expect a long meal with many courses and conversation focussing on the food (and probably football). In the evening, Sicilians like to meet in the city's piazzas, enjoying a gelato or downing an Aperol Spritz on a bar terrace,watching the world go by.

Appearances matter here, and Sicilian homes will typically be perfectly clean and neat, especially when receiving guests. Sicilian dialect has many words to express this: *azzizzare* (to beautify) comes from Arabic; *orfanità* is Spanish-Palermitan dialect for looking good; *spagnolismo* (Hispanicism) naturally means seeming better than you are. Critics claim that Sicilians remain sluggish citizens, subsidy junkies with little sense of self-help. Sicilians reply that power and prestige lie elsewhere. History has taught them to mistrust institutions.

The Mafia

The modern Mafia took root in Sicily in the 1860s, ostensibly to help the rural poor have their share of the land reform and other benefits from Unification. In effect, the Mafia became an integral part of the island's power structure, controlling business and the workings of government.

The Sicilian flag with the Trinacria

Don't leave Sicily without...

Discovering Sicilian Baroque. Take in the beauty of Sicily's Baroque gems. The area comprising Noto, Scicli, Modica and Ragusa is a Unesco World Heritage site, with churches and palaces created in a wildly theatrical style, characterised by fantasy and ornamentation.

Experiencing a smouldering volcano. Take a trail-bashing jeep tour up Etna. Offshore, you can hike up Vulcano as it smoulders, or view the exploding cone of Strómboli from the sea.

Visiting some of the finest Greek temples in the world. Sicily has more ancient Greek temples than Greece. The most magnificent are at Agrigento, Segesta and Selinunte; on summer nights, they stage open-air Greek drama performances.

Tasting Sicily's sweet delights. Stemming from their Moorish past, Sicilians have a passion for sweet desserts and confectionery. There are *pasticcerie* galore displaying tempting cakes and pastries, including the mouthwatering ricotta-filled *cannoli* and *cassata siciliana*. The local favourite, *frutti alla Martorana*, are brightly coloured, calorie-loaded peaches, apricots, strawberries and cherries made of pure marzipan. They take their name from the church of La Martorana, where the Benedictine nuns first created them.

Taking a stroll in the capital Palermo. Both a glorious assault on the senses and the glittering summation of Arab-Norman artistic achievement, Sicily's capital packs a powerful punch with exotic architecture and vibrant street life – and the recent pedestrianisation of some of the historic centre only adds to the pleasure.

Exploring the island's wild landscape. The Zíngaro Nature Reserve is a stretch of gorgeous unspoilt coastline, skirting idyllic bays and rocky headlands. The Madonie Mountains are popular with hikers, offering fabulous views and lofty medieval villages to discover.

Falling in love with its glittering mosaics. Sicily is mosaic heaven. The Byzantine-Norman mosaics in Palermo's Palatine Chapel and in the cathedrals of Cefalú and Monreale are breathtaking. The Villa Romana has unrivalled floor mosaics.

Taking in a puppet show. Puppet shows are a Sicilian tradition. Their stories are based on the adventures of the knights in Charlemagne's court.

By the 1970s, Sicily had emerged as a strategic centre for drugs, arms and international crime. In the early 1980s, a Mafia war left Palermo's streets strewn with blood and the Corleone-based clan undisputed

Taormina's Teatro Greco

Castellamare and coastline

Hikers on Etna

victors. In response to charges of government complicity, a crackdown on the Mafia was launched. Thousands of suspects were rounded up and an anti-Mafia pool of magistrates was assembled. One 'maxi-trial' resulted in 18 life sentences. Two Mafia-fighting magistrates, Giovanni Falcone and Paolo Borsellino, were murdered by the Mafia in 1992. The terror continued in 1993 with bombs in Milan and Rome, and an explosion at Florence's Uffizi Gallery.

The atrocities weakened the Mafia's grip on public opinion, its greatest weapon, and dented the age-old code of loyalty.

The new Sicily

No one could pretend that Cosa Nostra has disappeared. Its influence is still shaping politics and it is more often than not seen as the cause of Sicily's economic problems. But in response to changing circumstances the Mafia has abandoned high-profile terror for money-laundering, arms-dealing, drug-trafficking, protection rackets, embezzlement of EU funds and property speculation. Where once Mafioso activity was seen as revolt against the state, justified by centuries of foreign oppression, today Sicilians are less tolerant of organised crime, particularly the young.

The confiscation of Mafia property continues apace, and the Addiopizzo grassroots movement fights against the payment of *pizzo* (extortionate protection money). Since it was founded in 2004, hundreds of businesses across Sicily have signed up. Civic-minded Sicilians also support Libera Terra shops and cooperatives, which sell pasta, oil, cheese and wine produced on confiscated Mafia land.

For the islanders, the activities of the Mafia are not the only ongoing woes. Apart from its budget deficit, Sicily faces one of the highest unemployment rates in Europe and an unprecedented wave of emigration, including many of the brightest young Sicilans. Since the late 1990s, Sicily and the small island of Lampedusa to its south, have been a gateway for the influx of immigrants from North Africa and the Middle East. Tourism attracts an increasing number of visitors to the island spurred in part

Ornate balcony, Noto

Top tips for exploring Sicily

Hiking up Etna. Independent hikers can choose one of the two main routes up Etna: the northern route via Linguaglossa, considered cooler and prettier in terms of scenery, with forests and wild flowers. The southern route, via Nicolosi, is more dramatic with the barren flanks of the volcano scarred by lava flows and gritty fields of clinker. Jeep and trekking trips include hikes around summit craters, the black and desolate Valle del Bove, scene of the main eruptions, the underground lava cave of Grotta del Gelo (Dec–May) and the 2002 eruption zone. Winter hiking in high areas is not possible due to snow and bad visibility.

Sicilian markets. A foray into the raucous and exotic street markets, especially in Palermo and Catania, is a great experience. You'll find everything from slabs of swordfish and live eels to hunks of parmesan, salted capers and sun-dried tomatoes to cheap clothes and crafts. Every Sicilian town of any size holds a market at least once a week.

Aeolian Islands. Visit these tiny volcanic islands by boat from Milazzo on the north coast of Sicily. They all have their own character whether it's smouldering Volcano, spectacular Stromboli or chic Panarea. Visit on a day's excursion or base yourself in Lípari and ferry hop across to the smaller islets.

Chocolate box. Módica is famous for its chocolate, which is very sweet, slightly gritty and comes in all sorts of flavours. You can sample it, along with an irresistible range of cakes and pastries, at Bonajuto at Corso Umberto I No. 159, down a side street almost opposite the church of San Pietro. As well as chocolate bars there are *impanatigghi*, pastries made with chocolate and meat (not that you'd know), *testa di Moro*, fried pastry filled with chocolate custard, and *cannoli* pastries, filled with sweet ricotta cheese and chocolate.

Catania by bus. If pushed for time in Catania, consider the hop-on-hop-off, multi-language bus tour (www.katanelive.it) which costs just €5.

Summer festivals in Taormina. The tourist office in Palazzo Corvaja provides information on all the seasonal cultural events at the Greek Theatre. The Taormina Film Festival in July is one of the highlights of the year, drawing big international names.

by the restoration of Baroque towns – particularly the Unesco-listed gems of southeast Sicily – and the creation of nature reserves to protect areas of outstanding beauty. Chic boutique and luxury hotels, country house villas and wine estates are also part of the exciting new Sicilian landscape.

Hop On Hop Off Bus

Capella Palatina mosaics, Palermo

Food and drink

The food alone makes a trip to Sicily worthwhile. The island's Arab heritage, fertile volcanic soil and teeming seas have supplied the islanders with a rich and varied cuisine. This is complemented by an impressive selection of wines.

One of Sicily's best-kept secrets is its cuisine. Only a few local dishes, such as the sweet-and-sour aubergine side dish known as *caponata* or ricotta-filled *cannoli*, have crossed the Strait of Messina to find fame and fortune abroad.

The Greek colonists who arrived in the 8th century BC were astonished at the fertility of Sicily's volcanic soil, and Siracusa soon became the gastronomic capital of the Classical world. By the 5th century BC the city had given birth to the first cookbook written in the West (although only one recipe survives) and also to the first school for chefs.

The Arabs set the mould of Sicilian cooking, introducing aubergines, citrus fruits and rice, along with a sweet and spicy cuisine. Cane sugar was introduced, as was the Middle Eastern taste for sumptuous sweets – still a classic Sicilian trademark.

Until the Renaissance, the island exported pasta, sugar, confectionery and citrus to northern Italy. But while the Spanish brought chocolate and tomatoes from the New World and French chefs refined the raw ingredients, Sicilian cuisine reflected class lines. The poor survived on bread, beans, broth, and wild greens, the nobility dined on lavish 'baronial cuisine' from plates of gold and silver. The cooking typical of Sicily today is a combination of the traditions of the rich and poor, but always dedicated to exalting the extraordinary flavours of the produce.

Local cuisine

Palermo relishes a blood-and-guts cuisine, with such staples as *milza* (spleen) and chicken giblets. In western Sicily, Arab influences prevail, both in Trápani's *cuscus* and in dishes made with pine nuts and raisins. Agrigento prides itself on its *coniglio all'agrodolce* – sweet-and-sour rabbit with aubergines, capers, olives and wine. Around Etna, specialities include pasta with wild mushrooms and herby sausages, while in the hilly interior salami and cow's cheeses are common.

Where to eat and drink

Traditionally a *ristorante* is smarter and more expensive than a *trattoria* or *osteria*, but these days there is little difference between them. Pizzerias are plentiful. The best use wood-fired ovens

Fresh anchovies, Catania market

(forno a legna), but these are sometimes open only in the evening. A *tavola calda* or *rosticceria* are both café-style eateries where hot dishes are prepared daily.

Cafés and bars are a way of life for Italians, from the breakfast *cappuccino* and *cornetto* to the lunchtime snack and coffee to the evening *aperitivo*. In summer, Sicilians will start their day by dipping a soft Sicilian *brioche* in their coffee-flavoured *granita* (crushed ice). Along with wines and often a remarkable range of cocktails and liqueurs, bars also serve pastries, bread rolls, sandwiches and other snacks. An *enoteca* (wine bar) will offer a platter of sliced *prosciutto crudo*, salami or cheese to accompany its wide choice of fine wines.

What to eat

Antipasti (starters)

For starters Sicily offers an array of vegetables, from peppers in oil *(peperonata)* to stuffed tomatoes *(pomodori ripieni)*. Aubergines are a staple, whether grilled, fried, rolled and stuffed *(involtini di melanzane)* or baked in a parmesan and tomato sauce *(melanzane alla parmigiana)*. Fish starters, ranging from marinated anchovies to octopus salad are also popular.

A classic dish is *caponata*, featuring fried peppers, aubergines, tomatoes, courgettes, celery and olives. The sea provides inspiration for the classic *insalata di mare*, a seafood salad tossed in a dressing of oil, lemon and herbs, and *pesce spada affumicato* (smoked swordfish).

Il primo (first course)

Under the Arabs, Sicily was the first place to produce dried pasta on a commercial scale. The best-loved dish is *pasta alla Norma* (after the heroine in the opera by native son Bellini). Here tomatoes, basil, fried aubergines and a sprinkling of salted ricotta melt into a magical blend. Equally famous is *pasta con le sarde*, legendarily invented in the 9th century by Arab army cooks who used whatever was at hand: sardines, saffron, pine nuts, dried currants and sprigs of wild fennel.

Pasta is served with a wide variety of seafood, from clams *(alle vongole)* and sea urchins *(ai ricci)* to prawns *(ai gamberi)* and cuttlefish ink *(al nero di seppia)*. Pasta can also be paired with *fritella*, a spring sauté of new peas, fava beans and tiny artichokes, or simpler combinations garnished with sautéed courgettes. In the Trápani area, where the Arab influence is strongest, a local version of couscous, steamed in a fish broth, supplants pasta. This is best tasted during the vibrant September Couscous Festival at San Vito lo Capo.

Il secondo (main course)

Fish and seafood predominate in Sicily and, apart from in the interior, are generally a better bet than meat. On the coast, fresh grilled fish, mussels and

Sicilian wine

Olives are a staple

risotto marinara (seafood risotto) are rarely bettered. *Sarde a beccafico* – filleted sardines stuffed with cheese, garlic, parsley and capers – are on most menus. For simpler tastes try a grilled swordfish steak *(pesce spada)* or tuna *(tonno)*. The mountain pastures of Madonie and Nebrodi produce exceptional lamb and pork. Beef is best stuffed and braised in tomato sauce or skewered and grilled *(involtini alla siciliana)*. In the interior, *impanata* is a popular pie with goat or lamb in a parsley and garlic sauce. *Incasciata* is made with sausage, broccoli, raisins, garlic and pine nuts.

Contorni (vegetables)

Vegetables in antipasti are nearly always delicious, but cooked vegetables and mixed salad are usually very simple – a green or mixed salad, and a choice of steamed seasonal greens maybe dressed with olive oil, garlic and chilli. *Peperonata* and *melanzane alla parmigiana* (see under *Antipasti*) reign supreme. Orange and fennel salad is a legacy of the Arabs; artichokes come fried, stuffed, roasted on coals, or braised with oil, parsley and garlic. The interior boasts a survivor from Classical times, *maccu*, which is a purée made from dried fava or broad beans flavoured with oil and wild fennel seeds.

Street food

Sicily has a long tradition of cheap snacks eaten on the hoof, especially in Palermo and Catania. Chickpea fritters and bread *(pane e panelle)*, potato croquettes, with anchovy and *caciocavallo* cheese *(crocchette di patate)*, grilled goat's intestine filled with onions, cheese, egg and parsley *(stigghiola)*, fried rice balls filled with chopped meat and peas *(arancini)*, and beef spleen or tripe roll *(pani cu'la meusa)* provide a movable feast of typically local taste. Look for food trucks in Palermo and Catania.

Food markets are the best sources of street food, especially in Palermo and Catania. Street snacks can also be seriously sweet: Enna's speciality of *le sfingi* (rice-flour doughnuts drenched in honey) or the ubiquitous *cannoli* (see under *Dolci*). Ice creams and *granite* (water-based ices) have always been good, but can now be spectacular – look out for gelateria offering seasonal flavours in imaginative combinations.

Dolci (desserts)

The Arab inheritance is reflected in spicy fruit jellies, sorbets and *cassata siciliana*, a cloyingly sweet sponge cake with almond paste and candied peel. In general, Sicilian patisserie is elaborate in appearance and sophisticated in flavour, combining the taste of citrus fruits with sweet cheeses, dried fruit and almonds. *Cannoli* are crisp, sweet, tube-shaped pastries stuffed with ricotta and candied fruit. It's the classic island favourite and can be found in every *pasticceria* along with *pasta reale* (marzipan fruits) and *pasta di mandorle* (almond cakes). Fruit, ricotta, honey,

Sicilian pastries are a speciality

almonds and pistachio nuts often flavour cakes and ice cream. Ice cream is a reason for pride among Sicilians: made with fresh fruits and usually no preservatives, the low-fat Sicilian gelato is said to have been invented by the Arabs who mixed snow from the peaks of the Etna with fresh fruit and sugar, and is more delicate in flavour than Italian gelato. A traditional August dessert is *gelo di melone*, a watermelon jelly pudding with chocolate seeds.

Drinks

Vino (wine)

Sicilian wines have a great pedigree, dating back to Phoenician and Greek times, and reached their heyday in the late 18th century when the English created Marsala. The non-fortified and dessert wines have traditionally underperformed. With their prodigious sugar content, they were dispatched north for blending to bump up the strength of better-known wines.
But in the last two to three decades tables wines have improved out of all proportion with a trend towards quality not quantity. The best red wines tend to be based on the local Nero d'Avola grape variety; look out too for the dry red Cerasuolo di Vittoria from Ragusa province, and the fashionable reds and whites from the lava-enriched foothills of Etna. *Trattorie* will often sell house wines in jugs, available by the *litro* (litre), *mezzo* litro (half-litre) and *quarto di litro* (quarter-litre). The wine varies hugely but can be surprisingly decent, and will cost a good deal less than branded wines – often less than a can of Coca Cola. Ask for the *vino della casa*.

Sicily's best-known wine is still Marsala. It's often mistakenly synonymous with cheap, sickly-sweet liqueurs (see page 57), but the best (known as *Vergine* or *Riserva*) are excellent dry, smooth, sherry-like wines. Sweet elixirs, in fact, are something of a Sicilian speciality. The island of Pantelleria produces Moscato di Pantelleria Naturale, made from Zibibbo grapes, while the island of Salina has a similar tradition but with Malvasia rather than Moscato vines, and Taormina produces Vino alla Mandorla, a wine made from crushed almonds.

Soft drinks

For a sure-fire remedy for the effects of summer heat try a *spremuta*, a freshly squeezed juice made with oranges *(arance)* or lemons *(limoni)*. Another refreshing Sicilian speciality is *granita*, a drink of crushed ice flavoured with the fresh juice of lemons, strawberries, other seasonal fruits or sometimes even sweetened coffee. Try mulberry *(mora)*, peach *(pesca)* or watermelon *(anguria)*. Sicilians also like to drink *Chinotto*, a dark-coloured, slightly bitter, carbonated soft drink produced from the fruit of the myrtle-leaved orange tree, which is only cultivated in the Taormina area.

Shopping

Sicily may not be as chic as mainland Italy, but that's part of its charm. Pottery, puppets, papyrus and coral jewellery represent the best of traditional Sicilian handicrafts, while volcanic rock and sulphur crystals make excellent souvenirs.

Although Sicily has a luxury designer mall (see Fashion), shopping on the island is less about Gucci or Armani and more about atmospheric street markets, ceramic workshops, black lava souvenirs and gastronomy. The best shopping is in Palermo, Catania and Taormina. In Palermo head for the shops around Piazza Verdi and Via della Libertà, in Catania the main shopping precinct is Via Etnea.

There are food temptations wherever you go: chocolate from Módica, pastries from Noto, pistachios from Bronte and capers from the Aeolian Islands. These make great gifts for people back home.

Shopping Hours

Traditional opening times are Mon–Sat 8/9am–1pm and 4–7.30pm, but many shops now stay open all day, without closing at lunch time. Non-food shops are mostly closed on Mondays and, with the exception of supermarkets, food shops usually close on Wednesdays. In Taormina, and most other major tourist centres, many of the shops are open every day in the high season.

Antiques

Siracusa is renowned for its reproductions of Classical Greek coins. Palermo offers treasures, fakes and junk at its daily flea market on Piazza Peranni tucked away behind the cathedral, while the shops around Corso Umberto sell a mixture of antiques and bric-a-brac. In antiques markets what you see is rarely genuine.

Some of the most distinctive items in antiques shops are parts of the painted carts *(carretti siciliani)* that were once the mainstay of transport in the countryside. Intact carts are now collectors' items.

Pottery and ceramics

Sicilian terracotta pottery dates back to Classical times, but the sophisticated Persian glazing techniques were introduced by the Arabs in the 9th century.

Today the best ceramic workshops are found in Santo Stefano di Camastra on the north coast and in Caltagirone, southwest of Catania. Santo Stefano sells a range of ceramics, but the authentic ware has a rustic look, often with fish motifs. Caltagirone ceramics

Kitsch souvenirs

have instantly recognisable animal and floral motifs in dark blue and copper green with splashes of yellow. Look out for the tall *albarelli* jars once used for storing dry drugs, and the vast selection of heads depicting characters from Sicilian history that are used as ornaments or flower pots.

Papyrus

The ancient Egyptians brought the African plant of papyrus to Siracusa, and Fonte Ciane near the city is now the only place in Europe where it grows wild. Stalls and shops all over the town sell inexpensive papyrus pictures, mostly copies of Egyptian designs.

Crafts

Erice produces bright, hand-woven cotton rugs. Monreale is known for straw and cane goods. Palermo, Catania and Taormina are home to jewellers selling coral and gold.

You can buy replicas of the puppets from Sicily's popular puppet theatres – puppetry's main traditions are in Palermo and some of the best models are still made there.

Food and Wine

Look out for delis selling local specialities such as fruit preserves, almond spreads, spicy pesto, salted tuna roe *(bottarga)*, honey, olive oil and salted capers. Sicilian pastries such as *cannoli* (see page 18) and almond cakes are abundant. Seasonal sweets and biscuits include marzipan lambs for Easter and *ossi dei morti* (dead men's bones) biscuits for All Souls. In Palermo, *pupa a cera* are figures made of icing sugar. A green tangerine fruit syrup from a Catanese *ciospo* (kiosk), or a pistachio pesto from a speciality shop, can make unusual gifts.

Local wines can be tasted in an *enoteca* (wine shop), which acts as a regional showcase. In Taormina you'll find the local *vino alla mandorla* (sweet wine flavoured with almonds) as well as dessert wine, especially Moscato and Malvasia from the volcanic islands.

Fashion

Sicilia Outlet Village (www.siciliaoutletvillage.com) in Agira, on the motorway just east of Enna, is Sicily's first luxury designer shopping mall. Fashions here are heavily discounted. In summer shuttles run from some of the main centres. For fashion elsewhere head to the boutiques of Taormina, Palermo (Viale della Libertà and Via Ruggero Settimo) or Catania (Via Etnea). Here you'll find designer clothes from Valentino, Coveri, Gucci, Armani and the half-Sicilian Dolce & Gabbana.

Anti-mafia shopping

Libera Terra (www.liberaterra.it), which farms land confiscated from the Mafia, sells produce such as wine, oil and preserves at its shops throughout Sicily.

Pottery maker in Santo Stefano

Antiques and bric-a-brac

Entertainment

Catch a concert or puppet show in Palermo, an alfresco classical drama in a Greek theatre, or listen to live music in Catania's late-night bars. For a quiet evening just enjoy the passeggiata (evening stroll) and a glass of Marsala in a local bar.

Palermo and Catania offer a great season of opera, ballet and concerts (see page 120). Catania suits a young crowd, with its late-night bars and live music venues. Palermo empties on summer evenings, when the locals decamp to the beach resort of Mondello for the nightly fashion parade and fine dining. For the most sophisticated nightlife, head to glitzy Taormina and join the chic set over cocktails at the grand hotels. If your visit coincides with one of the many festivals, be sure to leap in and cast inhibitions aside.

Classical drama

Sicily's classical theatres often return to their original function as great settings for ancient Greek drama. Between May and June different dramatic cycles are performed in the Greek amphitheatres, from Siracusa and Segesta to Selinunte, Agrigento and Morgantina. In Taormina, the Greco-Roman theatre (see page 83) is the spectacular setting for an annual summer arts festival in July and August which includes classical drama as well as opera, dance and music.

Film

Sicily has a fascinating cinematic heritage. Major movies featuring Sicily include *The Godfather* trilogy, *Cinema Paradiso* (1988), *The Leopard* (1963), based on Giuseppe di Lampedusa's eponymous bestseller, *Il Postino* (1994), *Strómboli*: *Terra di Dio* (1949) and more recently the Montalbano films and TV series, based on novels by Italy's bestselling author, Andrea Camilleri.

In the Footsteps of The Godfather is one of the most popular trails from Taormina and can be done independently with a visit to the villages of Forza d'Agro and Savoca, where *The Godfather* was filmed. In Palermo you can book a tour of the Teatro Massimo, where the melodramatic massacre in *The Godfather III* was filmed. The Montalbano Trail in the southeast takes you to towns and seaside spots which feature in the detective series. Ed: If room we could add the box on Montalbano and The Godfather from RG Sicily.

Festivals

Sicily has festivals for every season. A matter of great local pride, these are a

Teatro Massimo, Palermo's opera house

mix of pagan and Christian, magic and music, folklore and feasting. *Carnevale* marks the beginning of Lent and a period of abstinence but is celebrated in many places with licentious abandon.

Easter sees the most activity and is celebrated with processions of holy relics, re-enactments of the Passion or respects paid to Our Lady of the Sorrows. In Enna on Good Friday, 2,000 hooded penitents from medieval fraternities hold a silent procession; in Trápani the Easter procession tours the town for 20 hours non-stop. Palermo's glittering festival of U Fistinu in July celebrates the patron saint, Santa Rosalia, with six days of processions, fireworks and general mayhem.

Among the secular celebrations are Piazza Armerina's Palio dei Normanni, a medieval pageant (mid-August), Palermo's ice cream festival, Sherbeth (November) and Módica's Chocobarocco (usually December) – a chocolate extravaganza.

Puppet theatre

Travelling puppet shows have been a form of entertainment in Sicily for centuries. The tales are in Italian and are usually based on the exploits of knights in Charlemagne's court, but even if you don't understand Italian there's plenty to enjoy. Puppets are exquisitely painted and dressed and some, at 1.5m (5ft) tall, are almost life-size. In Palermo the Museo Internazionale delle Marionette (see page 40) regularly stages performances, and Figli d'Arte Cuticchio (www.figlidartecuticchio.com) presents reinterpreted versions of traditional puppet theatre. The Teatro Magno puppet theatre (www.mancusopupi.it) was opened in 1928 by Enzo Mancusi and his legacy lives on through the work of his grandson. Puppet plays can also be seen in Acireale, Catania and Siracusa. Travelling puppet shows tour the island in summer; ask at local tourist offices for details.

Nightlife

Catania celebrates a vibrant arts scene, offering a rich summer program of classical, live jazz and blues concerts. The nightlife is the best in Sicily, with a profusion of trendy galleries, bars, restaurants and clubs. As an energetic university city, Catania offers events ranging from pop-rock spectaculars to open-air summer festivals. The venues vary from converted refineries to cosy clubs in the city centre. Palermo's nightlife is less developed and some of the areas where the bars and restaurants are located are not particularly safe at night. The safest and liveliest piazzas are Piazza Castelnuovo and Piazza Verdi. In all of the smaller towns, it is traditional to spend the evening in the main piazza, usually in front of one of the bars, whereas clubs are often slightly out of town.

Puppet show in Siracusa

Tribute to Francis Ford Coppola, Savocca

Outdoor activities

Sicily holds increasing appeal for active visitors. The diversity of landscape, from mountains and volcanoes to tiny islands and beaches, is unmatched by other Mediterranean islands and provides myriad opportunities for active pursuits.

Coasts, islands and mountains lend themselves to year-round sporting activities. You can hike in the hills and mountains, explore the undersea world, quad bike on Etna, wade through gorges and explore offshore islands. For the adventurous there are hikes up active volcanoes – with nightly fireworks in the case of Strómboli. Along with skiing and hiking, Etna now offers gorge-trekking, mountain-biking, motorbiking and bone-shaking jeep ascents.

Beaches

Unlike Sardinia, Sicily is by no means overrun by swathes of soft sand – some of the best bathing is from coves or rocks, with deep water for snorkelling and diving. The offshore islands have lovely, often volcanic beaches, notably on Ustica, the Egadi and Aeolian Islands. Beaches south of Siracusa are wild and unspoilt, while those between Catania and Taormina tend to be rocky and exciting – though not ideal for swimming or young children. The sea is delightful from May to October, but out of season (November to March) rough waters may bring debris ashore. In high season the easily accessible beaches in the main resorts, particularly on the north coast, are invariably packed.

Water Sports

Rich in flora and fauna, the coasts are excellent for diving and snorkelling, especially off the rocky shorelines on the smaller islands and along the northern coast.

Ustica, home to a natural marine reserve, has spectacular diving in deep water around the remains of a wreck. Isola Bella, a tiny island off Taormina, as well as Marettimo on the Egadi Islands, are favourites with snorkellers and divers. The Aeolian Islands are perfect for sailing, but mainland Sicily is not well equipped for sailors. The best spots for windsurfing are on the south coast where a strong, dry wind often blows.

Hiking

Sicily's rugged terrain offers some great opportunities for hiking, and most of the nature reserves have marked trails. Increasingly popular

Trekking in the Alacantara gorge, near Etna

regions are the Nebrodi and Madonie mountains, both of which offer challenging hikes. In the Madonie trails ascend to the peak of Pizzo Carbonara (1,979m/6,495ft), and the mountains here have rich limestone flora with many rare species.

The Riserva Naturale dello Zíngaro (see page 48) is the most well-designed reserve, with trails along the coast via tiny coves with crystal waters, and paths cutting through forest-covered mountainsides. The volcanic landscapes of Etna exert an obvious pull for hikers, but it's advisable to take a guide and to wear sturdy shoes. (See page 87 for information on exploring Etna.) The Alcantara gorge also provides fascinating hiking adventures, both in-water and around the gorge itself, whose geometric rocky formations were formed by runoff from Mount Etna. The Aeolian and Egadi islands offer excellent opportunities for hiking, from climbing the craters of Vulcano and Strómboli to off-the-beaten track exploration of remote Filicudi or Marettimo. Summer heat often becomes unbearable from 11am, so hikers should start early in the morning.

Skiing

Sicily is not renowned for skiing, but Etna and the Madonie have basic facilities. The season normally runs from December to March.

Etna's ski resorts are Linguaglossa on the northern side and Nicolosi on the southern side. Both resorts are suitable for intermediate and expert skiers, but Linguaglossa is the better choice for beginners. The views are spectacular, and of course there is an element of bravado in the idea of skiing on a live volcano.

In the Madonie mountains, the main ski resort is the alpine village of Piano Battaglia.

Cycling

Sicily's steep terrain offers a challenge for cyclists, but demand has risen from visitors in recent years. Typical bike tours offered by agencies include Etna, the Val di Noto, the Marsala coast or the offshore islands, where cycling is particularly popular (perhaps because it's flatter) and reflects the slower pace of life. Most of the offshore islands have mountain bikes and e-bikes to rent.

Golf

Sicily has a handful of golf resorts, the most luxurious of which is Verdura Golf & Spa Resort, near Sciacca (www.roccofortehotels.com). The most established club, Il Picciolo (www.ilpiccioloetnagolfresort.com), is an 18-hole, par-72 course on the slopes of Mount Etna. The terrain is pretty challenging, and play can be suspended if lava flows threaten to reach the course.

Hiking up on Vulcano

Culture and history

Sicily's great source of fascination is the range and quality of monuments that illustrate its complex history. The classical temples, Moorish palaces, Swabian castles and Baroque palazzi lend a theatrical and unique presence to the island.

Sicily's history is a cavalcade of invasion by ancient tribes. The Sicani, Siculi and Elymni were the first settlers; then came the Carthaginians and Greeks, the Romans, Arabs, mercenaries and slaves, Vandals, Goths, Saracens, Normans and Spaniards. Most remained for long periods, adding rich layers to Sicily's extraordinary fusion of genes and culture. Of the three great ancient civilisations that held sway in Sicily, the Greeks left the most enduring architectural legacy. The Carthaginians' buildings and artefacts were largely destroyed by the Greeks, and little remains of Roman temples and public buildings.

Early settlers

In the 9th century BC, seafaring Phoenicians colonised northwestern Sicily from the island of Mozia, which retains its Phoenician port and sacrificial burial grounds. The Phoenicians soon came into conflict with Greeks who were tempted to Sicily by its fertile lands, trade and supply of slave labour, settling on the east coast at Naxos in 734 BC.

From their colonies in Siracusa and the east coast, the Greeks spread across the island. Siracusa became the cultural capital of the ancient world and the supreme power of Sicily, while the Dorian Greek colonies of Agrigento and Selinunte were two of the richest cities, their temples testifying to their wealth and grandeur.

Romans, Arabs and Normans

The Romans treated Sicily as a Greek treasure trove, breadbasket and an imperial playground. They may not have matched the lovely sites of Magna Graecia, but the Romans built temples and public buildings and left a legacy of sumptuous mosaics. A tantalising glimpse of Sicily as the playground of rich Romans is the Villa Romana at Casale (see page 67), where mosaics illustrate a phantasmagoria of bathing, dancing, fishing, hunting, music and drama.

After the fall of Rome, Siracusa briefly became the capital of Byzantium, and by the 9th century Arabs, Berbers and Spanish Muslims added a patina in the form of Moorish palaces, Arab imagery and freedom

Greek ruins in Selinunte

of worship. The Arab hallmarks were engineering, irrigation, the introduction of sugar cane and cotton, as well as coral- and tuna-fishing. Palermo was by now the most cosmopolitan city in Europe.

Arab liberalism paved the way for the Norman golden age, a period of expansion, enlightenment, prosperity and cultural riches. Count Roger, an itinerant Norman knight, captured Palermo in 1072 and ruled Sicily as an oriental sultan, as did his son Roger II. The cities were graced by Arab-Norman churches and ringed by palms, vineyards, citrus groves and silk farms. Palermo's jewel box, the Cappella Palatina, and the cathedrals in Monreale and Cefalù display the fusion of Arab and Christian, and reflect the Norman inheritance.

A descendent of Roger II, Frederick II von Hohenstaufen (1194–1250), King of Sicily and Holy Roman Emperor, was one of the most brilliant rulers in medieval history. A man of remarkable culture and ability, he introduced a unified legal system, was a patron of science and the arts, and spoke six languages fluently. He wrote poetry and a book on falconry, and studied science, pondering such arcane questions as the workings of Mount Etna and the precise location of hell. Called Stupor Mundi, the Wonder of the World, his legacy to the island is, however, no more than a few forbidding royal fortresses.

Spanish rule

Almost five centuries of Spanish rule followed, when Sicily was isolated from the European mainstream. The aristocracy acquired a taste for *spagnolismo*, the pomp and circumstance associated with Spain.

After a devastating earthquake in 1693, much of eastern and southern Sicily was rebuilt in the Sicilian Baroque style. The eastern Baroque was sober – a mood underscored by the dark lava-stone churches – but that in the south was theatrical and symmetrical, while Palermitan Baroque was sumptuous, in the Spanish style.

From Unification to the present

A period of unrest, when Sicily once again became a pawn of foreign powers, set the stage for Garibaldi's campaign to liberate Sicily from the Bourbons and begin the Unification of the Kingdom of Italy. However, Italian independence brought little benefit to Sicily, merely exchanging the Bourbon viceroys for bureaucrats in Rome.

The Allied occupation of Sicily in 1943 was another grim episode, one that unwittingly encouraged the revival of the Mafia by bringing Mafia bosses from New York to raise Sicilian help in defeating the Germans. Huge swathes of unregulated building fattened Mafia coffers. These days the vast majority of Sicilians take an anti-Mafia stand, and lands confiscated from the Mafia are being used for the common good.

Arab-Norman mosaics in Monreale

Sumptuous Baroque in Palermo

Chronology

'Sicily is the schoolroom model for beginners, with every Italian quality and defect magnified, exasperated and highly coloured.' This view by the Italian commentator Luigi Barzini is supported by the bewildering legacy of Sicilian history.

Early history

20,000–10,000 BC Cave dwellers settle on Sicily.
c.1250 BC The Siculi (Sicels), Sicani (Sicans) and Elymni (Elymians) settle.
c.860 BC Carthaginians establish trading posts at Panormus (modern Palermo), Solus (Solunto) and Motya (Mozia).
c.733 BC Corinthian Greeks found Siracusa.
730–700 BC Greek colonies created at Megara Hyblaea, Gela, Selinus (modern Selinunte) and Akragas (Agrigento).
5th century BC Peak of Greek civilisation. Siracusa rivals Athens in power and prestige.
264–241 BC First Punic War ends in Roman domination of Sicily.
212 BC Siracusa falls to the Romans.
AD 395 Sicily passes to the Western Roman Empire.
468 Start of barbarian invasions.
535 Byzantines retake Sicily for the Empire.

Medieval Sicily

831 Palermo falls to the Arabs.
End of 8th century Sicily under Arab control. Arab colonisation ushers in a golden age for Sicily. The new capital, Palermo, becomes a prosperous centre of scholarship and art, second only to Constantinople.
1061 The Normans land in Sicily: the struggle against the Arabs.
1071 Norman Count Roger de Hauteville takes Palermo 'for Christendom'.
1130 Count Roger's son, Roger II, becomes King of Sicily.
1198–1250 Hohenstaufen Emperor Frederick II expels Arabs and rules Sicily.
1266 Charles of Anjou is crowned king and conquers Hohenstaufens.
1282 Sicilian Vespers uprising ousts the French and installs the Spanish.

Spanish rule to Unification

1442 Alfonso V of Sicily takes Naples.
1669 Etna erupts, destroying Catania and east coast towns.
1693 Massive earthquake strikes the east, destroying all the towns of the Val di Noto.
1713 Treaty of Utrecht. Victor

Relief of Count Roger

Amadeus II of Piedmont-Savoy becomes King of Sicily.
1734–1860 Spanish Bourbons rule Sicily through viceroys.
1806–15 British occupation of Sicily.
1848–9 Sicilian Revolution.
1860 Garibaldi and his men land at Marsala and defeat the Bourbons.
1861 Sicily joins the newly declared Kingdom of Italy.
1890 Catania inaugurates the Teatro Massimo Vincenzo Bellini.

Modern Sicily

1908 Messina destroyed by an earthquake, with 80,000 victims.
1915 Italy joins the Allies in World War I.
1943 Allied invasion of Sicily.
1946 Sicily is granted regional autonomy.
1951–75 One million Sicilians emigrate, especially to the United States.
1986 The Mafia maxi-trials *(maxiprocessi)* indict hundreds.
1992 The Mafia assassinate two judges Falcone and Borsellino.
1995 Giulio Andreotti, seven times Prime Minister of Italy, faces charges of collaborating with the Mafia.
2010 In Palermo, Pope Benedict XVI preaches against the Mafia.
2013 Pope Francis I visits Lampedusa to commemorate thousands of migrants who have died crossing the sea from North Africa. The new airport of Comiso is inaugurated.

Giorgia Meloni

2014 Mount Etna erupts several times in dramatic fashion.
2017 Regional elections in Sicily see the victory of a centre-right coalition with Silvio Berlusconi at the helm. Salvatore 'Totò' Riina, notorious Sicilian Mafia boss serving 26 life sentences, dies aged 87.
2020 Italy is the first place in Europe to be hit by COVID-19,.
2022 Right winger Giorgia Meloni becomes Italy's first female prime minister.
2025 Pope Francis, head of the Catholic Church, dies on the 21st of April. The new pope, Leo XIV, is announced on 8th May.

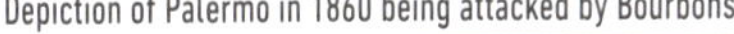

Depiction of Palermo in 1860 being attacked by Bourbons

TRIP PLANS

WALK 1
Western Palermo

Exotic Arab-Norman architecture and a vibrant street market dazzle the senses on this day tour of Palermo. From the Baroque heart of the city the walk takes you through the ancient Albergheria quarter, and on to Palazzo dei Normanni, with its glittering Palatine Chapel.

DISTANCE: 3km (2 miles)
TIME: A full day
START: Quattro Canti
END: Cattedrale
POINTS TO NOTE: Binoculars – or failing that, your smartphone zoom – are useful for the mosaics in the Cappella Palatina. The light in the chapel is constantly changing. Best times to go are late afternoon (as per the itinerary) or mid-morning. Watch your valuables in the Ballaro market, and take care if walking in the streets around Casa Professa at night.

Chaotic and gritty, Sicily's capital is a patchwork of periods and styles. In the Middle Ages, when Arab, Norman and Hohenstaufen rulers held sway, it was one of the most prosperous and enlightened cities in the Mediterranean – a melting-pot for Latin, Byzantine and Islamic cultures. Today the historic centre fuses ancient splendour with modern poverty and chaos. Pedestrianisation is slowly transforming this part of the historic centre – Quattro Canti is now traffic free, as are Via Maqueda, Corso Vittorio Emanuele (as far as the Duomo) and monumental piazzas such as Pretoria and Bellini.

After decades of neglect, Palermo is on the up; churches, museums and palaces have recently undergone or are undergoing restoration, cultural centres and galleries have opened, and the long–neglected seafront has been rebuilt with a proper promenade and gardens.

Get your bearings at **Quattro Canti** ❶, the heart of the city where the 'four corners' of the old centre are formed by two great arteries, **Via Maqueda** and **Corso Vittorio Emanuele**. After decades when heavy traffic made admiring the noble crossroads a life-risking activity, you can now scrutinise and photograph its symbolic Baroque statuary and fountains at leisure.

Piazza Pretoria

The Baroque **Piazza Pretoria** ❷ was once disparagingly nicknamed *Piazza della Vergogna* (Square of Shame), after the abundant saucy nudes who frolic in

Piazza Pretoria statue

the fountain's spray. This magnificently restored Mannerist pool, designed in the mid-1500s, has over 30 naked or near-naked tritons, nymphs and river gods of varying size and quality.

The piazza is overshadowed on one side by the huge domed church of **Santa Caterina**, where confectionary is sold from **La Dolceria** 1, and on the south side by the **Palazzo delle Aquile**, the town hall named after the stone eagles which decorate its facade.

La Martorana and San Cataldo

Further along Via Maqueda, **Piazza Bellini** 3 is graced with the three little red domes of the chapel of San Cataldo and the 12th-century campanile of **La Martorana** 4 (charge). Founded in 1143 by George of Antioch, King Roger's Syrian emir, the church is a remarkable mix of Baroque and Arab-Norman. The emir planned La Martorana as a mosque, yet adorned it with Greek Byzantine mosaics: one depicts the founder, while another shows Christ's Coronation of Roger II. Today, La Martorana is the co-Cathedral of the Catholic Church of Byzantine rite in Sicily, serving an Albanian ethnic minority. The Church of **San Cataldo** 5 (charge), a simple cube topped by red domes and flanked by palms,

Palermo Cathedral

is one of the last sacred buildings built in the Arab-Norman style.

Follow the signs outside Santa Caterina to the cloisters and join the queue for coffee and traditional – and tooth-achingly sweet – Sicilian pastries such as a Triumph of Gluttony made by nuns.

The Albergheria Quarter

Extending south and west of Piazza Bellini are the streets and alleys of the old **Albergheria** quarter. Its dilapidated houses and graffitied streets – now home to a vibrant, if occasionally edgy, multicultural community, were once the stomping ground of Norman court officials and wealthy merchants. Go south along Via Maqueda from Piazza Bellini, and take Via Ponticello, the first turning on your right. On Piazza Casa Professa the **Chiesa del Gesù** ❻ (free) was founded in the late 16th century as the first Jesuit church in Sicily, its interior a swirl of Baroque excess, including city's most exquisite and intricate inlaid coloured marbles.

Follow signs for the **Mercato di Ballarò** ❼, Palermo's liveliest daily market. Every morning except Sunday, the stalls fill Piazza Carmine, the adjacent Piazza Ballarò and the surrounding streets. It is raucous, sprawling and exotic, with the spicy scents and sounds that transport you back to Moorish times. There are mountains of lemons and oranges, slabs of tuna and swordfish, and a plethora of basic street-food stalls whose owners fight a losing battle with the flies attracted by the displays of ready-to-grill meat and fish.

After exploring the market, take Via Porta di Castro running west from Piazza Ballarò. Nearing the end of the street, turn left along Via Generale Cadorna and first right into Vicolo San Mercurio. If you are hungry stop for a meal at the peaceful **Eremiti** Osteria di Sicilia, see ❷.

San Giovanni degli Eremiti

At the end of the street cross the busy Via dei Benedettini for **San Giovanni degli Eremiti** ❽ (charge), distinctive for its five red cupolas. This ruined Benedictine abbey lies amid gardens of orange and mandarin trees, hibiscus, jasmine and acanthus. Built in 1132, it incorporates a Norman-Arab church, with a simple unadorned interior, the hall of an earlier mosque and delightful Norman cloisters planted with palms and kumquat trees.

Palazzo dei Normanni

Just north of San Giovanni degli Eremiti lies the Palazzo Reale, the eclectic royal palace, or the **Palazzo dei Normanni** ❾, as it is generally known. Centre of power since Byzantine times, it is now seat of the Sicilian Parliament. The Christians razed the Roman fort, the Arabs imposed a Moorish castle, remodelled by the Normans and later embellished

Chiesa del Gesù splendour

by the Spanish. Under both the Arabs and Normans, the palace was one of the most splendid courts in Europe.

Cappella Palatina

Little of the Arab-Norman palace remains, but one exquisite remnant is the **Cappella Palatina** ⑩ (Palatine Chapel; www.federicosecondo.org; charge), the royal chapel built for Roger II between 1130 and 1140 and one of the great highlights of a visit to Sicily.

The interior, akin to a jewel–encrusted casket, displays glittering mosaics on every surface. The oldest are those in the cupola and apse, designed to recall the life of Roger II as well as depict biblical scenes. **Christ Pantocrator** (Christ the All-Powerful), encircled by angels and saints, glimmers in the cupola. The chapel represents the fusion of Byzantine, Arab, Norman and Sicilian civilisations and harmoniously combines the three different styles. Greek, Latin and Kurif (early Arabic) script adorns the walls and capitals, a reminder of the languages of the Norman court. Arab craftsmen created the exquisitely carved and painted **coffered ceiling**, a panoply of Middle Eastern splendour. The Normans commissioned them to portray paradise; the Arabs gleefully conjured up naked maidens, which the rather prudish Normans clothed and crowned with haloes. Still, the roof remains a paradise of the senses: Persian octagonal stars meet Islamic stalactites. Hunters and revellers languish amidst palm trees entwined with dancers and female musicians; beyond, additional female musicians float into an *Arabian Nights* fantasy.

Royal Apartments

A marble staircase leads from the chapel to the **Royal Apartments**, once home to Spanish viceroys. As the seat of the **Sicilian Regional Parliament**, the visiting hours are limited (www.federicosecondo.org; guided tours; charge), worth a visit if only for the splendid **Sala di Re Ruggero** (King Roger's Salon), adorned with exotic 12th-century mosaics depicting lions, deer and peacocks set among palms and citrus trees.

From the ground floor of the palace you can descend underground to see the remains of the ancient **Phoenician-Roman walls** of Palermo, and the frescoed **Sala Duca di Montalto**, the setting for art exhibitions.

Cattedrale

Turn left out of the Palazzo dei Normanni and go down Via del Bastione following the bastions for **Piazza della Vittoria** ⑪, with its lawns and lofty palms. The Corso Vittorio Emanuele on the far side will bring you to the **Cattedrale** ⑫ (www.cattedrale.palermo.it; cathedral free, charges for Treasury, Crypt, Royal Tombs and Roof).

Built in 1185 but not completed until 1801 when the dome was added,

Lively Ballarò market

Food and drink

❶ La Dolceria (I Segreti del Chiostro)

Santa Caterina, Piazza Bellini; www.monasterosantacaterina.com/dolceria; €

Sicilian convents have been famed for their excessive desserts for centuries, and at Santa Caterina the tradition continues. Come, hungry, to sample crazy confections of vanilla custard, pistachio cream, candied fruit and rum-soaked sponge.

❷ Eremiti

Vicolo S. Mercurio 26; 329 867 7551; €€

Close to the eponymous church, the terrace/garden of this family-run restaurant/pizzeria/bar is an oasis away from the fracas. They do a very good lunchtime deal, with *pannelle*, pizza and a soft drink, or try the wonderful *paccheri* (big pasta tubes) with a sauce of Datterino tomatoes, almond, basil and crumbled sausage.

❸ Bisso Bistrot

Via Maqueda 172A; http://bissobistrot.it; €€

From the outside it looks like an old bookstore and that's what it used to be. Today it is a small, bustling bistro with a hip vibe, hearty helpings and reasonably-priced Sicilian specialities. Come for coffee, an *aperitivo*-hour glass of wine or for a full meal. Arrive by 7.15pm or be prepared to wait.

the building is a Sicilian hybrid: the 12th-century towers are Norman, the facade and south porch are Gothic, and the interior, after the golden, mostly medieval facade, is coldly neoclassical. The main entrance is a beautiful Gothic porch that includes a column with an inscription from the Koran. The church is a pantheon of the Normans, with six royal tombs on the left of the main entrance. The finest tomb was destined for Roger II, but Frederick II expropriated it. Roger now rots in a humbler tomb while his daughter, Queen Constance, lies in the sarcophagus on the far right. In the 1700s, the Cathedral was used as a solar 'observatory', and also features a bronze line on the floor known as *meridiana*, whose ends mark the positions as at the summer and winter solstices. Don't miss the Treasury, with Constance of Aragon's bejewelled crown, and do make sure you choose a ticket that includes access to the roof – a marvellous opportunity to see the city from on high. Afterwards, take a wander (or if the morning market is in swing, a shuffle and squeeze) through the **Il Capo quarter**, the setting for the city's most popular market.

For dinner in the vicinity, return to the **Quattro Canti** for a coffee, glass or wine or something more substantial at **Bisso Bistrot**, see ❸.

Tranquil cloisters of San Giovanni

WALK 2
Eastern Palermo

Start the day with sumptuous Baroque oratories, then explore the ancient neighbourhood of La Kalsa. Following a visit to two of Sicily's most engaging art collections – one ancient the other contemporary – the day ends on Palermo's new seafront, Il Foro Italico.

DISTANCE: 3km (2 miles)
TIME: A full day
START: Oratorio di Santa Cita
END: Villa Giulia
POINTS TO NOTE: Consider booking tickets at Teatro Massimo, www.teatromassimo.it, which has a wonderful programme of opera, ballet and concerts (see page 120). A few safety tips to bear in mind: beware of pickpockets in the market and take care in the backstreets at night.

The restored oratories (Catholic chapels) at the start of the tour display exquisite stuccowork by Giacomo Serpotta. In his hands simple square chambers are transformed into theatres of irresistible grace and gaiety. These quiet oratories have surprisingly few visitors and feel off the beaten track.

In the southeast, La Kalsa is one of the most interesting parts of Palermo. In Arab times the emir lived in splendour here and during the Middle Ages it was the home of wealthy merchants. Today it is a picturesque, rapidly regenerating quarter, and a wonderful place to hang out at night as well as explore by day.

Oratorio di Santa Cita

Start the day at the **Oratorio di Santa Cita** ❶ (Via Valverde 3; charge), accessed via a Renaissance loggia with garden. Serpotta's art here is at its most exuberant, with walls literally overflowing with cherubs playing with scrolls, garlands, swags of fruit and military trophies. Spectacular scenes on the end wall depict the victory of the Christian fleets over the Turks at the Battle of Lepanto (1571).

As Paul Duncan, author of *Sicily*, observes: 'You can nearly hear the chortling, farting and giggling of the putti, the rustling of undergrowth, the crack of a bottom slapped, and the swish of drapery.'

Oratorio di Santa Cita

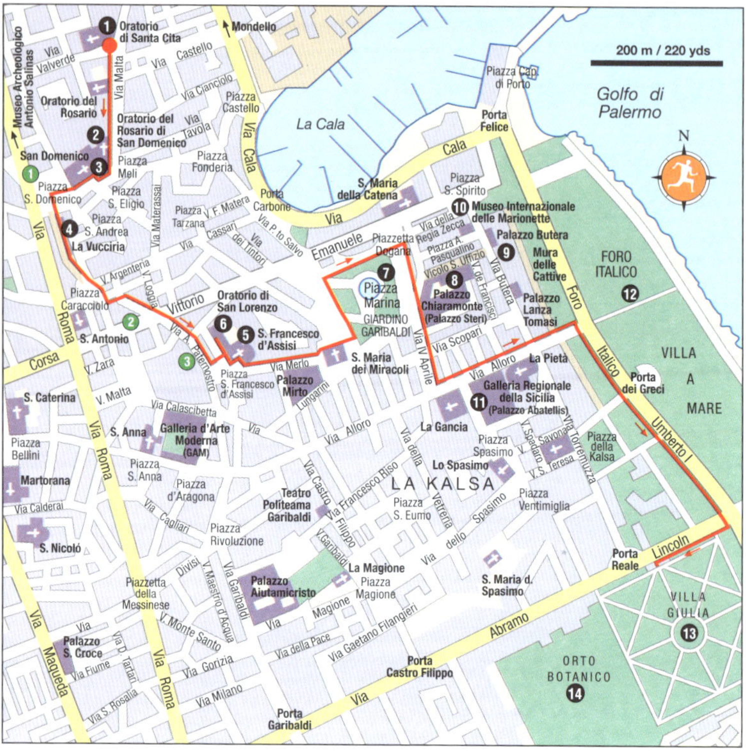

Oratorio di Santa Cita
Mondello
Museo Archeologico Antonio Salinas
Via Valverde
Via Castello
Via Malta
200 m / 220 yds
Piazza Cap. di Porto
Golfo di Palermo
Via Cianciolo
Piazza Castello
Oratorio del Rosario
Oratorio del Rosario di San Domenico
Via Tavola
La Cala
Porta Felice
Via Cala
San Domenico
Piazza Meli
Piazza Fonderia
Cala
N
Piazza S. Domenico
Piazza S. Eligio
S. Maria della Catena
Piazza S. Spirito
Piazza Tarzana
V. F. Matera
Porta Carbone
Museo Internazionale delle Marionette
Via
Piazza S. Andrea
Via Cassari
Via dei Tintori
Via P. to Salvo
Via della Regia Zecca
Palazzo Butera
La Vucciria
Via Materassai
Via Emanuele
Piazzetta Dogana
Piazza A. Pasqualino
Mura delle Cattive
Foro Italico
V. Argenteria
V. Loggia
Vicolo S. Uffizio
V. de Franciscis
Via Butera
Piazza Caracciolo
Vittorio
Oratorio di San Lorenzo
Piazza Marina
Palazzo Chiaramonte (Palazzo Steri)
Palazzo Lanza Tomasi
Foro
Roma
S. Antonio
Via A. Paternostro
S. Francesco d'Assisi
Giardino Garibaldi
Via IV Aprile
Via Scopari
Corsa
V. Zara
Via Merlo
S. Maria dei Miracoli
Via Alloro
La Pietà
Italico
Villa a Mare
S. Caterina
V. Malta
Piazza S. Francesco d'Assisi
Palazzo Mirto
Lungarini
Porta dei Greci
Galleria Regionale della Sicilia (Palazzo Abatellis)
Via Calascibetta
Via Alloro
La Gancia
Umberto I
Piazza Bellini
S. Anna
Galleria d'Arte Moderna (GAM)
Via della Vetreria
Piazza Spasimo
V. Spadaro
V. Savona
Via Torremuzza
Piazza della Kalsa
Via Roma
Piazza S. Anna
Lo Spasimo
V. S. Teresa
Martorana
Piazza d'Aragona
Teatro Politeama Garibaldi
Via Castro
Via Francesco Riso
La Kalsa
Piazza Ventimiglia
Via Calderai
Via Cagliari
Via Filippo
Piazza S. Euno
Via dello Spasimo
Piazza Rivoluzione
S. Nicolò
V. Garibaldi
Porta Reale
Lincoln
Divisi
La Magione
Via
Piazzetta della Messinese
V. Maestro d'Acqua
Via Garibaldi
Palazzo Aiutamicristo
Piazza Magione
Via Magione
S. Maria d. Spasimo
Villa Giulia
Via Maqueda
Via
Palazzo S. Croce
Via D. Tartari
V. Monte Santo
Via
Via della Pace
Via Gaetano Filangieri
Abramo
Via Fiume
Via Gorizia
Via Roma
Porta Castro Filippo
Orto Botanico
Via S. Rosalia
Via Milano
Porta Garibaldi
Via

Oratorio del Rosario di San Domenico

Turn right at the end of the road, crossing the square for Via Malta and Via Bambinai. The **Oratorio del Rosario di San Domenico** ❷ (charge) at No 16 is a Baroque jewel, another Serpotta oratory, where merchants worshipped in an interior encrusted with ornate seashells, angels and cello-playing cherubs. The Virtues that you see here were modelled on aristocratic Palermitan women.

The main altarpiece is a beautiful and impressive depiction of the *Madonna of the Rosary* (1628) by Van Dyck.

Puppet Theatre display

Around San Domenico

Turn right at the end of the street, past a cluster of jewellers, for **San Domenico** ❸ (charge), a Baroque church with an imposing twin-towered facade overlooking the piazza.

For a break from the Baroque and a spot of retail therapy or sustenance pop into the stylish **Rinascente**, see ①, on the square.

The Vucciria

From Piazza San Domenico follow your nose south down Via Maccheronai through the labyrinthine streets of the ramshackle **Vucciria** ❹ (Mercato La Vucciria see page 18).

This is Palermo's oldest market – made famous by a painting by Sicilian 20th century artist, Renato Guttuso but nowadays it is no more than a few modest stalls (the Capo [see page 34] has taken over as the city's number one market).

For lunch try the atmospheric **Casa del Brodo**, see ②, nearby on the main Corso Vittorio Emanuele.

La Kalsa

From **Corso Vittorio Emanuele** turn left and take the third turning on the right, Via A. Paternostro. On the little Piazza S. Francesco d'Assisi the **Antica Focacceria San Francesco**, see ③, is a Palermitan institution. The Church of **San Francesco d'Assisi** ❺ opposite has a splendid rose window and portal.

The nearby **Oratorio di San Lorenzo** ❻ (charge) has another Serpotta interior with lavish stucco decoration depicting the lives of St Francis and St Lawrence. Caravaggio's *Nativity*, featuring both saints, adorned the altar until it was stolen in 1969. Walk down Via Merlo for Piazza Marina.

Piazza Marina

Piazza Marina ❼, wraps itself around the **Giardino Garibaldi** where elderly Palermitani play dominoes and cards in the shade of banyan trees. The piazza is flanked by open-air bars and restaurants, and overlooked by handsome palazzi, including the **Palazzo Chiaramonte** ❽ (on the far side, also known as Lo Steri; www.coopculture.it; charge), a Catalan Gothic fortress that was a feudal stronghold before becoming the local seat of the Inquisition in 1598. Restored and open to the public, the complex includes a medieval Armoury, and the Sala dei Baroni with a remarkable 14th century wooden ceiling, every inch of it painted with intricate decorations, didactic exhortations and marvellous vignettes of courtly medieval life. Striking a very different note are the prisons where enemies of the Inquisition were incarcerated – including graffiti (some of it in English) made by the prisoners. Finally, don't miss the chance to see

Oratorio ceiling

Artisans in Vucciria Market

Antique treasures

A few blocks away from Santa Cita, the Museo Archeologico Regionale Antonio Salinas (Piazza Olivella 24; https://turismo.comune.palermo.it; charge), Palermo's Archaeological Museum, is housed in a late Renaissance monastery and displays one of the richest collections of Greek and Roman antiquities in Italy.

Most of the treasures come from the Sicilian sites of Tindari, Termini Imerese, Agrigento, Siracusa, Selinunte and Mozia. The highlights are the Classical finds from the temples at Selinunte (see page 59) displayed in the magnificent Sala di Selinunte. Stylised friezes portray Athena protecting Perseus as he battles with Medusa, Hercules slaying dwarves, Hercules and the Cretan Bull, Zeus marrying a frosty Hera and Actaeon attacked by his own dogs.

20th century artist Renato Guttuso's iconic La Vucciria market.

Just off Piazza Marina, on Via Butera, Palazzo Butera is home to the extraordinary contemporary collection of Massimo Valsecchi in **Palazzo Butera** ❾ (charge; www.palazzobutera.it) which opened in 2022 after a ground-breaking restoration project that had the international art world marvelling. The philosophy behind the palazzo is that visitors should come in and look at whatever draws them, whether it be the art or the palazzo itself, rather than seeking out the most famous works.

On the other side of Via Butera families will enjoy the **Museo Internazionale delle Marionette Antonio Pasqualino** (Puppet Theatre; Piazza Antonio Pasqualino; www.museomarionettepalermo.it; charge), which has an exotic collection of puppets. (see page 23).

Galleria Regionale della Sicilia

Take the Via IV Aprile south from the square for the Via Alloro, and turn left for the **Palazzo Abatellis**, home to the engaging **Galleria Regionale della Sicilia** ❿ (https://turismo.comune.palermo.it; charge).

The Catalan Gothic mansion and Renaissance loggia make a charming setting for Sicilian paintings and sculpture from the 15th and 16th centuries. The showpiece is the macabre but compelling 15th-century anonymous *Triumph of Death*: a skeletal grim reaper cuts a swathe through the nobles' earthly pleasures.

Other great treasures are Francesco Laurana's marble bust of *Eleanor of Aragon*, the Flemish Jan Gossaert's *Malvagna Triptych* (c.1520) and Antonello da Messina's *Annunciation*, a breathtaking portrait of the Virgin surprised at her reading by the Archangel Gabriel.

Orto Botanico

Food and drink

1 La Rinascente
Via Roma 289; www.larinascente.it; €€
The top floor with terrace of this stylish department store has a branch of the Obikà mozzarella bar, as well as other cool places to eat. In the early evenings hip Palmeritans hang out here sipping an *aperitivo* while watching the facades on Piazza San Domenico turn from tawny to violet.

2 Casa del Brodo
Corso Vittorio Emanuele 175; www.casadelbrodo.it; €€
This pleasantly old-fashioned restaurant started off in the late 19th century as a soup *(brodo)* kitchen and still remains in the same family. Based on ancient recipes, fava bean soup *(macco di fave)*, still features on the menu, along with other hearty, satisfying dishes such as *bucatini* pasta with sardines, and slow-cooked pork shank.

3 Antica Focacceria San Francesco
Via A. Paternostro 58; https://anticafocacceria.it; €€
Quaint, bustling and rough and ready, this place is something of a shrine for street food afficionados. Come here to try Palermitani specialities such as *pani ca' meusa* (strips of spleen, served with ricotta or *caciocavallo* cheese in a soft bun), *arancine* (fried rice balls) and *panelle* (chickpea fritters). Alternatively try one of the traditional home-style dishes such as pasta *alla norma* or pasta with sardines.

With a short detour, right behind the Galleria Regionale stands the former church and convent of Santa Maria dello Spasimo on Via dello Spasimo, which makes a charming setting for cultural events (see page 120).

The Foro Italico

Follow Via Alloro east in the direction of the **Foro Italico** 11. This was Palermo's grand seafront in the days of the Belle Epoque and a place for both public parade and louche encounters. The area fell into decline until the creation of the promenade.

The waterfront now features gardens and pathways, popular with joggers, cyclists, football-players and sunbathers, and stretches all the way to the gardens of the **Villa Giulia** 12 and the delightful **Orto Botanico** 13 (Botanical Gardens; http://ortobotanico.unipa.it; charge), a refreshing oasis full of tropical plants and shady walkways.

Foro Italico

WALK 3
Cefalù

Sitting snugly below a majestic headland, Cefalù is a picturesque family-friendly resort boasting a great cathedral, golden sands and a leisurely pace of life. Explore the alleys of the old quarter, climb the Rocca for bird's-eye views – or simply chill out on the beach.

DISTANCE: 3km (2 miles) including La Rocca (1 mile/1.5km without La Rocca)
TIME: A half-day walk
START: Piazza del Duomo
END: Seafront
POINTS TO NOTE: Frequent trains and buses link Cefalù with Palermo (70km [44 miles] away); both take about an hour and arrive at the railway station 10 minutes' walk from the centre. By car from Palermo take the route along the coastal SS113. The most central car park is Parcheggio Dafne (charge) on Via Aldo Moro, 10 minutes' walk from the sea front.

Cefalù is arguably the most charming resort on the Tyrrhenian coast. The medieval port retains its character, helped by a pervasive Arab atmosphere and a compact fishbone design which curls its way to the shore. The town may be a summer tourist trap (try to avoid July and August) and popular package tour destination, but the old quarter, with its narrow-cobbled alleys, retains its medieval air. For families in particular, Cefalù makes a welcoming base.

Il Duomo

Start the morning in one of the outdoor cafés on **Piazza del Duomo**, admiring the twin-towered facade of the Arab-Norman **Duomo** ❶ (Duomo free; charge for cloisters, roof and towers; https://duomocefalu.it/en). The cathedral, granted Unesco World Heritage Status in 2015, was built in 1131 by Roger II. The king had a sarcophagus made for himself, but he and his tomb are in Palermo Cathedral as he died before Cefalù's Duomo was completed. Inside, the austere nave is flanked by Roman columns spanned by slender pointed arches betraying Islamic influence, though your eyes will inevitably be drawn to the magnificent mosaics in between the stonework. Binoculars, opera glasses or your smartphone zoom are useful for seeing details. A social co-operative set up by the diocese organises excellent guided tours to the towers (80 steps),

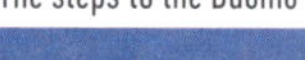
The steps to the Duomo

roofs and cloisters, and in August they often run special night-time visits.

Mosaics

Dominating all is the simple beauty of the mosaic of **Christ Pantocrator** in the apse, set above the Madonna, archangels and apostles. The All-Powerful's blessing is the standard Orthodox form: two raised fingers symbolise the duality of Christ's spiritual and temporal power, while the other fingers and thumb represent the Trinity. The left hand holds open the Bible with the Greek and Latin text (John 8:12) 'I am the light of the world.' In the purest Byzantine style this is the acknowledged masterpiece of Sicilian mosaic art.

Don't miss the incredible cathedral **cloisters** (chiostri; charge), to the left of the main entrance, and comprising three rows of elegant twin columns, with intricately carved capitals.

The Old Quarter

From the piazza, narrow alleys lead into the old town. The cobbled Via Mandralisca slopes down to the **Museo Mandralisca** ❷ (http://fondazione mandralisca.it; charge), one of

Duomo fresco

Cefalù beach

Food and drink

1 La Brace
Via XXV Novembre 10; www.ristorantelabrace.com; €€
This welcoming restaurant is excellent value and hugely popular. The menu offers specialities such as *involtini di pesce spada* (skewers of thinly cut slices swordfish wrapped around cheese and breadcrumbs), and a wonderfully sticky roast rabbit. There is a good choice of desserts. Book ahead.

2 Le Chat Noir
Via XXV Novembre 17; www.ristorantelechatnoir.it; €€
Despite the name, this family-run restaurant is dedicated to classic Sicilian dishes such as caponata, aubergine *parmigiana* and spaghetti with anchovies, home-made pistachio pesto, breadcrumbs and tomato.

Sicily's finest small museums and home to what may be the island's most enigmatic painting. The Renaissance *Portrait of an Unknown Man* (1465) Antonello da Messina is famed for the sitter's supercilious smile and Machiavellian expression. The collection was set up by Baron Mandralisca (1809–64), who discovered the portrait in a pharmacy on the Aeolian Island of Lípari.

From here explore the old quarter with its warren of alleyways and some appealing relics of Cefalù's past. At the end of Via Mandralisca turn left for the **Lavatoio Medievale** 3, where curved steps lead down to an arcaded Arab wash-house with cold river water. Take the Via Vittorio Emanuele north to the **Porta Pescara** 4, the old Arab port which has been a backdrop in countless films, including *Cinema Paradiso*.

Going back towards the cathedral, take Via XXV Novembre 1856, where you'll find two good restaurants: **La Brace**, see 1, and **Le Chat Noir**, see 2.

La Rocca

Above the medieval town and on the site of the original Arab town, **La Rocca** 5 (free) affords sweeping views over Cefalù and the sea. For the pathway up, head south along Corso Ruggero, then left along Vicolo Saraceni following the signs for Tempio di Diana. Allow two hours for the round trip if you are going right to the top, and beware that in summer it can be a sweltering slog. The Salita Saraceno climbs up three tiers of city walls to the restored fortifications of the crumbling stone castle, revealing traces of a pool, fountain, cistern and prison.

If La Rocca sounds too strenuous, head for the **beach** 6, one of the best in Sicily and hugely popular in summer. Parasols and sun loungers can be rented from May to September.

Cefalù skyline

TOUR 4

Monreale, Segesta and Zíngaro park

Leave behind the bustle of Palermo for the sumptuous Arab-Norman cathedral of Monreale and the evocative temple of Segesta. Discover the coastal paths of the Zíngaro Nature Reserve, then feast on fresh fish at Castellammare del Golfo.

DISTANCE: 106km (66 miles) plus walk in Zíngaro Nature Reserve
TIME: A full day
START: Palermo
END: Castellammare del Golfo (or Palermo)
POINTS TO NOTE: Wear appropriate dress for Monreale Cathedral – no short shorts or bare shoulders. Monreale is expensive for eating out and Segesta is a lovely spot for a picnic. Take swimming gear and walking shoes for Zíngaro Nature Reserve. The beaches are best avoided in midsummer.

Monreale Cathedral is the apogee of Arab-Norman artistic achievement and one of the wonders of the medieval world. According to a Sicilian proverb, *'He who goes to Palermo without seeing Monreale leaves a donkey and comes back an ass'*. The cathedral was the creation of the Norman King William II, who was known as William the Bad merely because he was slightly less popular than William the Good. From Monreale, the route heads southwest to the finely preserved Greek temple of Segesta, another cultural highlight, in a glorious, isolated setting. After a heady morning's sightseeing the afternoon is spent walking or chilling out on the north coast.

Monreale

Monreale ❶ is 8km (5 miles) from Palermo. From Piazza Independenza, just west of Palazzo dei Normanni, take the Corso Calatafimi and follow the SS186 for Monreale. Park in one of the signed car parks rather than the streets of the old town. There are no major sights other than the cathedral, but Monreale is an attractive little town for strolling, with narrow alleys, Baroque churches and an abundance of bars, restaurants and souvenir shops.

Cathedral facade

Set high above the Conca d'Oro valley and Palermo, the **cathedral** (http://monrealeduomo.it; cathedral free, charge to treasury and terraces,

Monreale cloisters

Monreale Mafia

Perched on a hill, Monreale enjoys fine views and after frenetic Palermo exudes tranquillity. Yet the town is home to the largest Carabinieri (police) barracks in Sicily, built after the Mafia murdered local officers in 1983–4. In 1996 the Archbishop of Monreale was himself investigated for Mafia collusion, extortion and fraud. Although perfectly safe, this touristy little town is reputed still to be a Mafia stronghold. From Monreale, rural roads lead south to the Mafia heartland of gulleys and mountain lairs. Nurtured by the mythology of banditry and the wartime cult of Salvatore Giuliano, Sicily's Robin Hood, the region remains insular.

north transept, Museo Diocesano and cloisters) was completed in just 10 years. Before entering, take time to look at the **Romanesque portal**, its delicate design inspired by Byzantine inlaid ivory, and the main **bronze door**, adorned with lions and griffins – royal motifs echoed by the Norman throne inside. The **apses** (seen from Via del Arcivescovado) are the most opulent in Sicily, with interlacing arches of limestone and lava, as delicate as wood.

Cathedral interior

Inside, the shimmering tapestry of mosaics is unequalled in Europe. Scholars dispute whether the **mosaics** are wholly Byzantine, finished by 1100, or completed by Venetians before 1250. Given Sicily's mongrel inheritance, it seems probable that they are a fusion of all the invading cultures. Islamic semi-lancet windows and arabesque decoration sit easily with Romanesque columns, marble details and Byzantine backgrounds.

On entry the eye is drawn to the imposing half-length figure of Christ Pantocrator in the central apse, with the enthroned Virgin and Child with angels and apostles below, and lower still, figures of saints. Above the arcade in the nave the luminous mosaics start with the **Creation sequence**. The loveliest of these 42 panels depict the creation of light, the world, the stars, fish and fowl. The Garden of Eden panels enshrine a Palermitan paradise, an orchard of exquisite fruit trees, flowers and exotic birds. Here, a matchmaking God presents a perky Eve to a sleepy Adam.

The Norman kings ruled by divine right, a message proclaimed throughout their cathedrals. Above the royal throne is a mosaic of **Christ crowning William II**, a tribute to a Christian king whose world view embraced concubines, eunuchs and black slaves. In the nearby side chapel William is buried in an elaborate marble sarcophagus.

Tower, terrace and cloisters

In the south of the nave, climb the **tower** (charge) for fine valley and

The cathedral's lofty interior

sea views, and from the **terrace** look down onto the splendid **Chiostro dei Benedettini** (Benedictine Cloisters), surrounding a courtyard garden.

The Romanesque cloisters not only express William's great love of Islamic art but also reflect the cosmopolitan nature of the Norman court. Craftsmen from Provence, Venice, Pisa, Greece, Africa, Persia and elsewhere in Asia all worked on Monreale. Not that the Normans were un-Christian: one sculpted pillar depicts William presenting the cathedral to the Virgin. Every second pair of white marble columns has a vivid zigzag mosaic spiralling up the shaft. A Provençal sophistication is suggested by the columns; by contrast, the Moorish mood is sensuous, evoked by rich mosaic inlays and arabesque carvings. The marble sculptures in the cloisters echo the mosaics but with a personal or secular note, from a mason's signature to an animated picture of tree-planting and pig-killing. A Moorish corner is enhanced by a loggia and a sensuous, slightly phallic fountain. Shaped like a palm–tree trunk, the shaft is crowned by lions' heads, as in Granada's Alhambra.

If lunch can't wait, a good option is **Taverna del Pavone**, see 1.

Cathedral statuary

Tonnara di Scopello

Segesta

From Monreale come down the hill, follow the SS186 towards Partinico, then north of the town join the A29 autostrada in the Trápani direction. Exit at Segesta. The journey takes about an hour.

Segesta ❷ (www.parcodisegesta.com; charge) is arguably the most eloquent of all Classical sites in Sicily. The temple and theatre, dating from the 5th and 3rd centuries BC respectively, stand on separate hilltops overlooking rolling countryside and sea – still wonderfully empty and isolated, despite the motorway.

The ancient settlement of Egesta (today's Segesta) is thought to have been founded in the 12th century BC by the Elymians, a race who occupied much of northwestern Sicily, but about whom little is known. The settlers had to switch allegiance frequently between Carthaginians and Greeks to ensure survival. They destroyed Greek Selinunte in 409 BC, but a century later, in 307 BC, Agathocles, tyrant of Siracusa, sacked Egesta, killing nearly 10,000 inhabitants and selling others into slavery.

Although one of the best-preserved of Italy's Doric temples, Segesta's **Temple** was never completed. Apart from no roof, the bosses, used for hauling up the stones into position, remain on the steps, the columns are unfluted and there are gaps in the bases of the columns. But it is no less lovely for that.

Walk – or take the shuttle bus -- to the **Teatro** on Monte Barbaro 4km (2.5 miles) away. In spring the hills are a riot of wildflowers and this makes a lovely walk. Excavations on Monte Barbaro are ongoing. The Arabs and Normans settled here and there are ruins of an ancient castle and church, but the main attraction is the well-restored Greek theatre cut out of the side of the mountain. With its views of the Golfo di Castellammare, it's a fine backdrop for Greek plays in summer.

Scopello

Return to the A29, direction Palermo, and exit at Castellammare del Golfo. Follow the coast road northwest following signs for **Scopello** ❸, a picturesque rustic hamlet which grew up around a 17th-century farmstead. Enjoy a drink in the main piazza, or a meal at **La Tavernetta**, see ②. Just east of Scopello, the Tonnara di Scopello (charge) is an old scenic tuna fishery on an irresistible little cove with sparkling blue waters. The fishery has been restored and part of it is now a B&B. Apart from peak season when, like every single one of Scopello's tiny rocky coves, it is seething with visitors, this is an idyllic place for a dip.

Zíngaro Nature Reserve

The **Riserva Naturale dello Zíngaro** ❹ (charge), sandwiched between

The theatre at Segesta

Food and drink

1 Taverna del Pavone
Vicolo Pensato 18, Monreale; tel: 091 640 6209; €€
This cosy, welcoming inn offers traditional dishes such as spaghetti with seafood, *pappardelle in a rich wild boar ragù and lamb chops with porcini mushrooms*

2 La Tavernetta
Via Armando Diaz 3, Scopello; www.albergolatavernetta.it; €€
Try the *busiate* (handmade pasta twists) with pistachio and prawns, fish couscous or the *tagliata di tonno* (fresh tuna, seared and sliced) at this popular hotel restaurant. It is family-run and has garden and sea views from the restaurant terrace.

3 La Cambusa
Via Don Luigi Zangara 67; Castellamarre del Golfo; www.ristorante-lacambusa.eu; €€
Watch the fishing boats and the local *passeggiata* as you tuck into all things fishy at this popular harbourfront restaurant. An extensive choice includes mussel soup, seafood pasta, smoked tuna, grilled squid and fish couscous.

mountains and sea, embraces a 7km (4.3-mile) stretch of gorgeous coastline, happily recovering after a devastating wildfire in 2020. The path hugs the coast, skirting secret coves, idyllic bays and rocky headlands, but there are also trails inland. The reserve is rich in flora, with yellow euphorbia, palms and carobs; it's also a haunt of buzzards, falcons and the rare Bonelli eagle. Access (on foot only) is a 2km (1.25-mile) drive from Scopello. The coastal path (Sentiero Basso) is well signed but facilities are scant.

The park could occupy an entire day, but if you're considering a short walk and a dip, take the path to Cala Capreria, a lovely cove with a small natural history museum, or it's another 20 minutes to Cala del Varo.

Castellammare del Golfo

Head for **Castellammare del Golfo** 5 in the early evening. Set on the eponymous gulf, near good beaches, this is an overgrown fishing village with a charming harbour below a squat Saracen castle, and fine views across the gulf. Dine at one of the fish restaurants at the harbour. At **La Cambusa**, see 3, you pay a bit extra for harbour views, but it's a lovely spot to sit outside (or behind large glass windows) and watch the world go by. Sitting here, it's strange to think that Castellammare was once a notorious Mafia haunt.

Castellamare beach

Castellamare harbour

WALK 5
Trápani and Erice

A lively port since Phoenician times, Trapani now has an elegant centre with revamped churches, palaces and seafront. On a mountain high above, exquisite Erice is the island's moodiest medieval town: lovely in any season, whether swathed in winter mists or a carpet of spring flowers.

DISTANCE: Walk in Trapani: 3.5km (2 miles); Trapani centre to Erice 12km (7.5 miles) by car, bus or cable car
TIME: A full day
START: Trapani centre
END: Erice
POINTS TO NOTE: For buses to Trapani from Palermo go to www.segesta.it, for trains www.trenitalia.it. The train and bus stations are about a 15-minute walk from the old centre. By car from Palermo take the A29 motorway. Trapani has its own airport at Birgi, 16km (10 miles) south of town with a bus service to City Terminal at Trapani. The Trapani/Erice cable car (www.funiviaerice.it) is closed in mid-winter and on Monday mornings. Pedestrians should consider purchasing the Trapani Welcome Card (www.trapaniwelcome.it), which lasts three days and allows unlimited travel on public transport, one return journey on the cable car to Erice, 50 percent off Castello Venere and other discounts.

Squeezed onto a narrow promontory on the west coast, Trapani was once the centre of trade for coral, tuna and salt with the Levant, Carthage and Venice. Today it is a fishing and ferry port, as well as an arrival point for budget airlines from Europe (and Italy).

Until quite recently Trapani was seen as a workaday city in which to kill time before the next ferry to the Egadi Islands. But it has changed: Baroque churches have been restored, the main Corso Vittorio Emanuele partially pedestrianised and the dodgy fishing quarter converted into a seafront promenade.

The sprawling modern outskirts are hardly welcoming and there are no great sites, but Trapani is certainly worth a visit for the old quarter, the salty port and the seafood eateries with their delicious fish couscous *alla trapanese* made with sea bass, sea bream, red mullet, grouper, mussels, clams and prawns, and a sprinkling of chilli.

Trapani beach

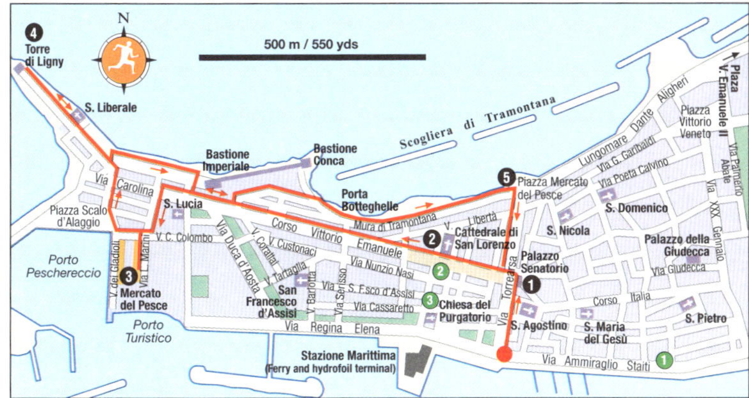

A world apart from Trapani, Erice makes a more peaceful base for exploring – and staying. Perched 750m (2,500ft) above the coast on a windswept isolated mountain, it is a small fortified medieval town. The sea views are staggering, and on a clear day you can spot the Egadi Islands and, according to the locals, even Cape Bon in Tunisia.

The city was founded by the Elymians, the mysterious settlers of Segesta who built a richly decorated temple dedicated to the fertility goddess known as Astarte (Aphrodite to the Greeks and Venus to the Romans). The mountain was much fought over, particularly by the Romans and Carthaginians. The Arabs called it *Gebel-Hamed*, Mohammed's Mountain, and Count Roger, who had visions of St Julian while attacking the town, renamed it Monte San Giuliano.

Trapani

The centre

The old town has an easy charm, with its 11th-century Spanish fortifications matched by a regenerated seafront. Set on a narrow curving promontory, it was formerly named Drepanon, the ancient Greek for sickle. This is where most of the sights are clustered. If you're feeling peckish, pop into **Angelino**, see 1.

Head inland along the elegant **Via Torrearsa**, the main shopping street, then west along **Corso Vittorio Emanuele**, which cuts through the 'sickle' and at its eastern end closes with a grand Baroque flourish at **Palazzo Senatorio** 1, the town hall.

Fishing boats in Trapani harbour

The Corso is flanked by fine balconied palaces and churches, including the imposing **Cattedrale di San Lorenzo** ❷ (free).

Follow the road to the end of the promontory, diverting slightly south for the **Mercato del Pesce** ❸ (Fish Market) next to the **fishing port**.

At the tip of the promontory, the **Torre di Ligny** ❹ (charge) is a squat Spanish fortress built in 1671, now restored and housing a small collection of archaeological finds hauled from the seabed. Softly illuminated, the tower now makes a romantic evening stroll – and there is good swimming from the rocky beach below.

Return to the centre via the ancient Spanish bastions on the north side of the promontory – there are steps from Porta Botteghelle for good views of the bay and fishermen's cottages. The seawalls here lead along to **Piazza Mercato del Pesce** ❺, site of the former fish market.

For lunch head back to Corso Vittorio Emanuele, taking Via Torrearsa south, and try the delicious home-made fare at **La Tavernetta Ai Lumi**, see ②, at No. 75; or authentic slow food at **La Bettolaccia**, see ③, north of the ferry terminal.

The modern town

The city's main monument, the **Santuario dell'Annunziata** ❻ (free) lies in modern Trapani, about 3km (2 miles) east of the old town. Drive east along the main Via G. B. Fardella and bear right at Via Pepoli, or take a bus from Piazza Vittorio Emanuele.

The Carmelite church, founded in 1315 but rebuilt in 1760, has a rococo nave and a cluster of exotic domed chapels. Behind the high altar is the lavish **Cappella della Madonna**, with the revered statue of the Madonna di Trapani by Nino Pisano, crowned in jewels. This venerated Madonna is credited with miraculous powers.

The **Museo Regionale Pepoli** ❼ (https://www2.regione.sicilia.it/beniculturali/museopepoli/museopepoli.html; charge), arranged around the beautiful

Erice castle

Porta Trapani, Erice

cloister of the former convent adjoining the cathedral, is the city's eclectic museum of regional sculpture, paintings and crafts.

Erice

The writer Carlo Levi called Erice 'the Assisi of the south, full of churches, convents, silent streets and mythological memories'. But this is no sanctuary, especially in summer. Orphanages and convents have been converted into cute craft shops or restaurants and, in midsummer, music festivals are held in the cobbled squares.

The town lies 10km (6 miles) northeast of Trapani. If driving, take the main Via G.B. Fardella, and follow the signs up to Erice. Buses depart regularly from City Terminal and the bus station at Piazza Montalto, taking the best part of an hour; the views are lovely, but better still is the **Funierice cable car** ❽ (www.funiviaerice.it), which takes just 10 minutes and affords wonderful views of saltpans, mountains, sea and islands.

Bitter almonds

In the 1950s Maria Grammatico, who owns the famous Pasticceria Maria Grammatico in Erice, was sent to an orphanage run by nuns. Her father had died of a heart attack and her mother, carrying a sixth child, could not cope alone with such a large family. Life was tough at the orphanage, but it was here that Maria Grammatico learnt to make the sweets and almond pastries for which she is now famed. Her melancholic girlhood recollections are recounted in her autobiography, *Bitter Almonds*, co-authored with long-time Sicilian resident, Mary Taylor Simeti.

The centre

Buses, cars and the cable car all arrive by the entrance to **Erice** ❾, the Norman **Porta Trapani**. Beyond the gate lies the Chiesa Madre, which is also the Duomo, (charge), the largest of Erice's 10 churches and founded by Frederick II; climb the campanile, Torre di Re Federico II (charge), for fabulous views.

Cloisters in Trapani

Pasticceria Maria Grammatico

Food and drink

1 Angelino
Via Ammiraglio Staiti 87, Trapani; www.angelino.it; €
This hugely popular café serves a range of reasonably priced dishes as well as irresistible cakes and pastries. Do as the Sicilians and tuck into the delicious *arancine* (fried rice balls filled with chopped meat and peas).

2 Ai Lumi
Corso Vittorio Emanuele 75, Trapani; www.ailumi.it; €€
Converted from the stables of an old palazzo, this is an atmospheric spot with some of the best food in town. The cuisine here is traditional Sicilian: succulent steaks, roast lamb and braised rabbit – also very fresh fish and seafood.

3 La Bettolaccia
Via Generale Enrico Fardella 25 (corner of Via Francesco d'Assissi), Trapani; www.labettolaccia.it; €€
Popular little osteria near the port. The *busate al pesto trapanese* (handmade pasta twists with a pesto of basil, almonds and fresh tomato) is as good as it gets.

4 Pasticceria Maria Grammatico
Via Vittorio Emanuele 14, Erice; www.mariagrammatico.it. €
This is Sicily's most famous *pasticceria*. Try the *cannoli*, marzipan fruits, *dolci di badia* (almond cakes), *mustaccioli* (chocolate and almond biscuits) – to name a few. Maria Grammatico also own the Caffè Maria with a panoramic terrace down the road at No. 4 and Antica Pasticceria del Convento in Piazzetta San Domenico.

Exploring the streets of the medieval town you will invariably spy sweet cakes and pastries. According to legend, Erice lived off *dolci ericini* made by nuns, and **Maria Grammatico**, see 4, is perhaps the most authentic bakery in Sicily.

Castello di Venere

Dominating the rocky outcrop at the top of the town lie the ruins of the **Castello di Venere** 10. The castle was built in the 12th century on the site of the Tempio di Venere, with blocks from the pagan temple being used for the walls.

From here there are staggering views, though if you come off season it may be shrouded in mist. Below the castle are the **Giardino del Balio** (public gardens), with an ivy-clad 15th-century tower and more glorious views from the garden terraces. Below stretch wooded groves and vineyards, and a tapestry of saltpans and sea out to the Egadi Islands and as far as Cape Bon in Tunisia.

View from Castello di Venere

TOUR 6

Along the African Coast

This seafaring region represents a swathe of ancient Sicily, from Phoenician Mozia to Greek Selinunte and Arab Mazara del Vallo. At Marsala you can taste the eponymous wine and visit a Punic ship.

DISTANCE: 88km (55 miles)
TIME: A full day
START: Trapani
END: Selinunte
POINTS TO NOTE: Set off early to allow plenty of time for Selinunte – or miss out Marsala or Mazara del Vallo. For information on ferries to Mozia, see www.mozialine.com or www.ariniepugliese.com.

The west coast of Sicily is often known as the African coast because it is closer to Tunisia than to mainland Italy, and its early settlers were Arabs from North Africa. The landscape spans dazzling saltpans, Marsala vineyards and coastal nature reserves.

The Salt Road (Trapani to Marsala)

Follow the narrow coastal road south of Trapani (SP21), where mountains of salt are signs of an industry that dates from antiquity. The **Museo del Sale** ❶ (Salt Museum, Núbia, 6.5km (4 miles) south of Trapani; charge, www.museodelsale.it) demonstrates salt production, and has an inviting *trattoria*.

Rejoin the coast road and follow brown signs for *Imbarco per Mozia* (also signed Mothia and Motya). This ancient Phoenician settlement lies on the tiny island of San Pantaleo, one of the **Isole dello Stagnone** ❷, a marshy trio of lagoon islands and now a nature reserve, home to wild ducks, pink flamingos, avocets and African cranes. From the Ettore e Infersa saltworks (www.seisaline.it), small ferries chug across to San Pantaleo. A little shop, the Bottega del Sale, in the finely restored salt windmill here sells pots of salt, either pure or flavoured with a tantalising range of herbs, citrus and other aromatics.

Mozia

Sicily's chief Punic site, **Mozia** ❸ or Motya as it was known, was a colony set within a ring of ramparts and towers. During the 8th century BC the Phoenicians colonised the west coast, from Marsala to Palermo and Solunto, and Motya was the first Sicilian outpost of this naval and trading empire. In

Saltplans at Nubia

398 BC Dionysius I, tyrant of Siracusa, besieged the town.

Motya was bought in the early 1900s by Joseph Whitaker, a wealthy English-Sicilian archaeologist and ornithologist who discovered Phoenician remains while inspecting vines on the island. The **Museo Whitaker** (www.fondazione whitaker.it; charge) displays Punic and Greek pottery, hundreds of burial urns, carved *stelae* and jewellery. The prize piece is a Greek statue from the early 5th century BC of a sinuous youth, ***The Man in a Tunic***. The ruins of Motya are still only partially excavated but you can still see remains of the city walls, the Punic dry dock and the **Tophet**, a sacrificial site where the Phoenicians worshipped sun, moon and fertility deities. The charred offerings of animals and jars containing burnt babies, sacrificed to the gods, were unearthed. Close to the museum the **Casa dei**

Fishmonger in Mazara

Mosaici has black and white pebble floor mosaics of exotic animals.

Marsala

Continue on the coast road to **Marsala** ❹ (12km/7.5 miles), famous for dessert wine (see box). Set on Sicily's most westerly cape, Marsala was originally a Carthaginian port called Lilybaeum, and derived its present name from the Arabic Mars-al-Allah, 'the port of God'. In the later Middle Ages it became the frequent victim of African-based pirate raids, and Trapani took over as the major trading port – except for wine.

Wine apart, Marsala is a pleasant town of Baroque buildings, lending itself to a leisurely stroll, a seafood meal and a glass or two of the local tipple. Sample a fine Marsala in one of the *enoteche* (wine bars) in Via Garibaldi such as **La Sirena Ubriaca**, see ①, or try a glass over a fish grill at nearby **Trattoria Garibaldi**, see ②. On 11 May 1860, Garibaldi, along with his Redshirts, landed at Marsala, freeing the island of the Bourbon regime and setting the stage for the Unification of Italy. Throughout Marsala you can see plaques to the famous freedom fighter.

Marsala wine

In 1773 English merchant John Woodhouse shipped 60 oak barrels of rich golden Marsala wine to England, having added a dose of alcohol to ensure it would survive the long journey. The wine was an instant success in England and was soon stocked instead of port by the British navy. Marsala later lost its reputation and was regarded as a cheap sweet liqueur, confined to cooking. Recent years, however, have seen a renaissance in quality, with producers making dry, smooth, amber dessert wines, aged in oak barrels and known as Vergine or Riserva. Leading producers include Florio, Donnafugata, Marco de Bartoli, Cantine Pellegrino, Cantine Martinez and Caruso & Minini, all of whom offer tastings.

Archaeological Park of Lilybaeum

Capo Boeo, the western tip of Sicily, is the city's archaeological zone. On the seafront, the **Museo Archeologico Regionale Lilibeo** (www.parcolilibeo.it; charge) displays ancient ruins from the city and a reconstructed 35m (115ft) long Punic warship discovered by an English archaeologist in 1971 in the Stagnone lagoon, and believed to have sunk off the Egadi Islands during the First Punic War in 241 BC. It doesn't look much, but it's the only surviving Punic warship and has provided invaluable information on life aboard in that era. The museum gives access to the **Insula Romana**, part of a Roman villa. The **Ipogeo di Crispia Salvia** (book in advance by calling 0923 952535 or e-mailing parco.archeo.lilibeo@regione.sicilia.it) reveals a subterranean chamber with fresco

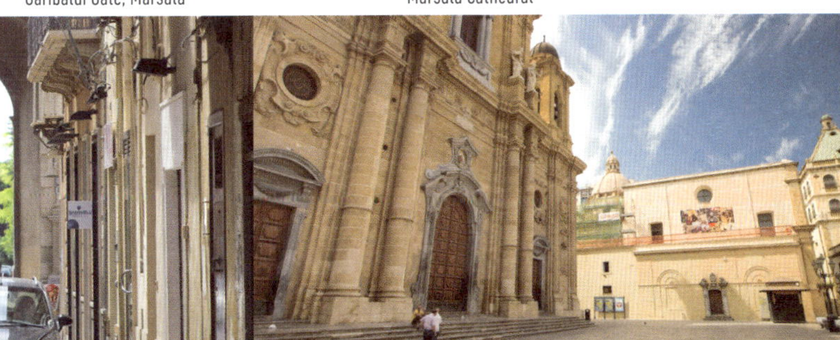

Garibaldi Gate, Marsala

Marsala Cathedral

fragments of funerary banqueting scenes.

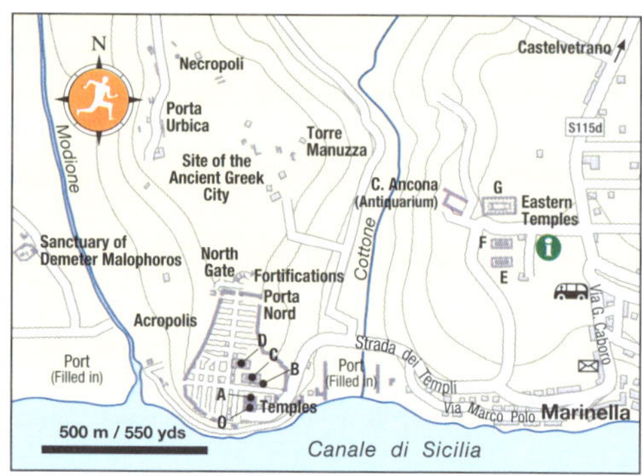

Mazara del Vallo

Take the SS115 24km (15 miles) to **Mazara del Vallo** ❺, passing by cube-shaped North African houses and miles of modern sprawl. Mazara may be of Phoenician origin but Arab influences predominate, from the Tunisian trawlermen to the Arab music and shisha pipes. However, the **Kasbah**, with its maze of backstreets, has been newly gentrified with freshly painted houses and ceramic plaques and murals. The town has a long and pleasant tree-shaded seafront, with marina and beach, and a centre of fine churches.

The evocative **Norman Arch**, near the seafront, is all that remains of Count Roger's castle. Across the palm-filled park lies the **Cattedrale** (Piazza della Repubblica; free, irregular hours), rebuilt in the 17th century but retaining Norman apses. From the square, Via XX Settembre takes you to the **Museo del Satiro Danzante** (charge), which displays a 4th-century BC bronze satyr recovered from the local seabed in 1997–8.

For lunch you could try Tunisian dishes at **Alla Kasbah**, see ❸, in the old town on the edge of the Kasbah.

Selinunte

Follow the SS115 east, turning off to Campobello and follow signs for **Selinunte** ❻. Founded by colonists in 628 BC, it took its name from *selinon*, the Greek for wild celery which grew here in abundance. By the 5th century BC it had become a prosperous city with over 100,000 inhabitants, great temples and two harbours. Inevitably the colony became embroiled in the battle between Athens and Phoenician Carthage and was sacked by Carthage in a nine-day siege in 409 BC. The citizens resettled in Marsala (Lilybaeum) and the site was abandoned.

Parco Archeologico

Selinunte's grace lies in its splendid isolated setting by the sea. The **Parco Archeologico** (www.coopculture.it/en/poi/selinunte-archaeological-park-cave-di-cusa-and-pantelleria.-archaeological-area-of-selinunte; charge) consists of

Temple ruins at Selinunte

Food and drink

❶ La Sirena Ubriaca

Via Garibaldi 39, Marsala; www.lasirenaubriaca.it; €

A good spot to sample Marsala and other wines, accompanied by crostini, olives and dips. The hosts of this small enoteca are multilingual and will guide you through the different Marsalas – it's not called the Drunken Mermaid for nothing.

❷ Trattoria Garibaldi

Piazza dell'Addolorata 35, Marsala; tel: 0923 953 006; €€

This popular trattoria in the centre has been keeping the locals happy and fed since the 1960s, and continues to offer a fine spread of seafood and vegetable antipasti, *pasta con le sarde* (sardines), fish couscous or simply grilled fish – or meat.

❸ Alla Kasbah

Via Itria 10, Mazara del Vallo; tel: 0923 906 125; €€

Popular with the locals, this is a bustling and atmospheric place for fish couscous, *busiate* (hand-made pasta twists) with prawns and a mixed antipasto.

four zones: the acropolis overlooking the sea, the ancient city on the hillside, the sanctuary of Malophorus, dedicated to Demeter, goddess of fertility, and the imposing eastern temples that visitors flock to see.

The temples

Since temple attributions are uncertain, they are identified, rather prosaically, with letters of the alphabet.

Begin with the **main temples** (E, F and G) on the eastern hill. Dating 480–460 BC and partly reconstructed in 1958, **Temple E**, possibly dedicated to Hera (Juno) and in pure Doric style, is the most dramatic and complete of the temples. **Temple F**, in ruins, is dedicated perhaps to Athena, while **Temple G** is a vast heap of ruins with one restored column rising from the rubble. It was one of the largest temples of Classical antiquity.

From here stroll along the Strada dei Templi to the **Acropolis**, with the remains of the oldest temples (**A, B, C, D and O**) and reconstructed walls. Nearest the sea are the elusive **Temples O and A** (480–470 BC).

The more conspicuous **Temple C**, with 14 standing columns and splendid sea views, is the oldest of the other three temples.

Marinella

A walk along the sandy beach of neighbouring **Marinella** ❼ makes a pleasant end to the day. The seafront at this modern resort is lined with lively restaurants, excellent for seafood.

WALK 7

Valley of the Temples, Agrigento

Dramatic ruins of one of the ancient world's greatest cities face the sea on the south coast of Sicily. The Doric temples in the Valle dei Templi rival the finest ancient ruins in Greece.

DISTANCE: 4.5km (3-mile) walk in the Valley of the Temples; 1km (0.6 miles) walk (or car, bus or taxi) to the Museo Archeologico Regionale; (optional 3km [2 miles] from museum to modern Agrigento).
TIME: A full day
START: Valley of the Temples
END: Museo Archeologico Regionale or modern Agrigento
POINTS TO NOTE: With just one day restrict your visit of the town of Agrigento to the evening. Take a picnic to the temples and consider splashing out in the evening at Villa Athena, reserving a table overlooking the temples. For full appreciation of the ruins, an audioguide or guided tour in English is recommended. Ask at the entrance for audioguides or book a guide ahead via www.lavalledeitempli.it/en/guided-tours. Beware that in midsummer Agrigento can be unbearably hot and crowded, but check the website for summer night openings, which are magical.

In its heyday, in the 5th century BC, Agrigento rivalled Athens in splendour. Known as Akragas, it comprised painted temples in a natural amphitheatre, a valley of wild thyme, silvery olive and almond groves. In the past, it was considered a sybaritic city, and Plato claimed that the people of Akragas 'built for eternity but feasted as if there were no tomorrow'.

Founded by colonists from nearby Gela and Rhodes on the south coast in 581 BC, the city prospered as a tyranny until it was sacked by the Carthaginians in 406 BC. After a Roman revival the site was destroyed by Byzantines, who razed all the 'pagan' temples except Concordia. Akragas was then abandoned until the 18th century.

Nowadays the valley remains evocative, even if the modern world intrudes with unappealing high-rise apartment blocks seen in the distance. Much of modern Agrigento is an unappetising urban mix, but it has a medieval core, well worth a visit if you have time at the end of the day.

Temple of Concordia

Cattedrale
San Giorgio
V. Duomo
Piazza Bibirria
Via Gioeni
V. Plebis Rea
Via Imera
Palermo
Santa Maria dei Greci
Purgatorio
Santo Spirito (Museo Civico)
Piazza Vittorio Emanuele
V. S. Vito
Via Cicerone
200 m / 220 yds
N
V. Atenea
V. Fodera
Palazzo Filippini
Via Atenea
Piazzale Aldo Moro
V. Empedocle
Via Minerva
San Calogero
Via Giovanni XXIII
Piazza Marconi
Stazione Centrale F.S.
Piazza Metello
Via F. Crispi
Viale della Vittoria
Via Dante
V. Esseneto
V. Callicratide
Via Venezia
Via Manzoni
Via F. Crispi
Stadio
Viadotto Akragas
Via U. la Malfa
Via Demetra
Museo Archeologico Regionale
Via Petrarca
San Biagio
10
San Nicola
2
Giardino della Kolymbethra
9
Hellenistic-Roman Quarter
Tempio Rupestre di Demetra (Rock Sanctuary of Demeter)
Via dei Templi
Valle dei Templi
Via Panoramica dei Templi
Hypsas
Temple of Hephaistus
Santuario delle Divinità Ctonie (Sanctuary of the Chthonic Deities)
Piazzale dei Templi
1
8
7
1
V. dei Templi
Café
Via Sacra
5 Tempio di Giunone (Temple of Juno or Hera)
Tempio di Dioscuri (Temple of Castor & Pollux)
6 Tempio di Giove (Temple of Jove or Zeus)
Tomba di Terone (Theron's Tomb)
3 Villa Aurea
4 Tempio della Concordia (Temple of Concord)
2 Tempio di Ercole (Temple of Hercules)
Gela
Tempio di Asclepio (Temple of Asclepius)
SS115
Akragas

Valle dei Templi

The arrival point of the **Valle dei Templi** (www.coopculture.it/it/poi/parco-archeologico-e-paesaggistico-della-valle-dei-templi; charge) is **Piazzale dei Templi** ❶, once the agora or marketplace. The archaeological park is divided into two sections: the Eastern Zone, with the main temples, and the Western Zone, linked by a walkway.

Start at the Eastern Zone where you purchase a ticket and follow the Via Sacra. The temples are transformed by light, and were praised by Lawrence Durrell in *Sicilian Carousel* as 'pure opalescent honey'. A local saying goes that you have not lived until you have seen the Temple of Concord change

with the seasons, at dawn, dusk and moonlight. Ideally, return after dinner to see the temples glow in the black countryside, radiating security and serenity before the Mediterranean Sea.

Eastern Zone

Tempio di Ercole

The first treasure is the **Tempio di Ercole** ❷ (Temple of Hercules), just within the enclosure. This was designed in the Archaic Doric style in 520 BC and, as such, is the oldest temple. It once protected a statue of Hercules and had a glorious entablature emblazoned with lions, leaves and palms. Today just eight columns from the original 38 rise up from the mound of rubble. These were re-erected in 1924 by Alexander Hardcastle, a devoted Scottish archaeologist, who lived at the **Villa Aurea** ❸, a short way up on the right.

Tempio della Concordia

Follow Via Sacra to the superbly sited **Tempio della Concordia** ❹ (Temple of Concord), which, after Theseion in Athens, is the best-preserved Greek temple in the world. The tapering columns tilt inwards, creating a lofty grace that belies the weighty entablature. The temple dates from 430 BC, but was saved from destruction during the 6th century AD, when it was converted into a Christian church. The temple still represents sheer perfection in line.

Tempio di Giunone

Cool off with an iced drink or *gelato* at the café on the left as you go up. At the end of Via Sacra stands the **Tempio di Giunone** ❺ (Temple of Juno, also known as Tempio di Hera), surmounting a rocky ridge. Part of the temple fell over the hill after a landslide, but the rest is well preserved. Juno was the goddess of marriage, and her shrine is the most romantic of temples. Yet in reality it was a ghoulish spot: the stones were tinged red after the temple was licked by Carthaginian flames in 406 BC.

The Western Zone

Tempio di Giove

With the area of a football pitch, the **Tempio di Giove** ❻ (Temple of Jove, also called Zeus Olimpico) was the largest Doric temple ever known, although it was never finished. The U-shaped grooves on the stone blocks are pulley marks formed during construction. Today's rubble is indecipherable: the masonry was plundered to build the harbour walls at Porto Empedocle, the outlet for Agrigento's sulphur and potash industries. Thirty-eight telamones (7-metre-high columns carved as male figures) were originally built into the walls between the columns, supporting the architrave, one of which has been re-erected. As well as their aesthetic and practical functions, the telamones

Temple of Hercules

had allegorical significance, illustrating the war against Zeus. Like Atlas, the defeated giants were compelled to carry the world on their shoulders.

Tempio di Dioscuri

West of the Temple of Jove (Zeus Olimpico) is a puzzling quarter dotted with pagan shrines. The **Tempio di Dioscuri** ❼ (also known as Tempio di Castore e Polluce, or Castor and Pollux) was named after Zeus' twin sons. Castor was mortal and Pollux immortal, so they spent alternate days in Hades and on Mount Olympus. Graceful and evocative, the ruin is in fact an artistic pastiche, erected in 1836 from the remains of other shrines.

Just behind lies what is believed to be the 6th-century **Santuario delle Divinità Ctonie** ❽ (Sanctuary of the Chthonic Deities), concealing sacrificial altars and well-like ditches. The sanctuary is a shrine to fertility, immortality and eternal youth.

Giardino della Kolymbethra

Close to the Sanctuary, climb down to the **Giardino della Kolymbethra** ❾ (combined ticket with Valle dei Templi, free to FAI National Trust members), a large and verdant garden of orange groves, along with almonds, olives, bananas and numerous other Mediterranean trees and plants. It began life as a vast pool, used originally for sacred rites and later for agriculture. It has been restored and provides a delightful diversion from the Temples and a perfect spot for a picnic, sitting on a bench under orange trees.

Museo Archeologico

A short drive or 1km (0.6-mile) walk up Via dei Templi from Piazzale dei Templi leads past **Villa Athena**, an eyesore of a hotel with sublime views from the restaurant, see ❶, to the Archaeological Museum, the Hellenistic-Roman quarter and a clutch of pagan shrines. The fortifications which you can see en route are a reminder that Agrigento was once enclosed by walls, towers and massive gates.

The **Museo Archeologico Regionale** ❿ (charge, combined ticket with temples) incorporates a church, courtyard and temple foundations, and a wealth of artefacts found during excavations at the Valley of the Temples. This is an excellent museum, with labels in English – you could easily spend half a day here. Highlights are the black and red Attic vases, the section on the Temple of Jove (or Zeus Olimpico) in Room 6, including temple reconstructions, a marble *ephebe* (classical youth) in Room 10 and the child's sarcophogus in Room 11.

If you're calling it a day you might consider an early seafood dinner at **Trattoria dei Templi**, see ❷, 300m/yds east of the museum.

Igor Mitoraj bronze sculptures, Valley of the Temples

Temple of Hera

Food and drink

1 Villa Athena

Via Passeggiata Archeologica 33; www.hotelvillaathena.it; €€€

This lovely five-star villa-hotel with restaurant scores highly on atmosphere and for magical views across the Valley of the Temples. La Terrazza degli Dei restaurant is the place for a romantic lunch or dinner on the terrace, with both *à la carte* and tasting menu options. Reservations advisable.

2 Trattoria dei Templi

Via Panoramica dei Templi 15; tel: 0922 403 110; €€

Fish and seafood dominate the menu at this vaulted, rustic retreat conveniently close to the temples and popular with tour groups. Fish of the day is always a good bet. Reservations advisable.

3 Ex Panificio

Piazza Giuseppe Sinatra; www.osteriaexpanificio.it; €€

Lovely place occupying the premises of a historic bakery where the focus is on carefully sourced ingredients. Try ravioli stuffed with local goat cheese, spaghetti with anchovies and breadcrumbs or *cavatelli alla norma* (wth tomato, salted ricotta and aubergine).

Modern Agrigento

Crowning the ridge to the north of the Valley of Temples, modern Agrigento occupies the site of the Greek Acropolis. Most visitors skip the city, deterred by the outlying sprawl, distance on foot from the temples or parking problems. However, there are buses from the Valle dei Templi, and it's a quick ride in a taxi.

The old part of town has a tatty medieval charm, though restoration has begun on a handful of historic buildings. The main **Via Atenea** is a pleasant street for strolling with plenty of restaurants, including the lovely **Ex Panificio** 3.

The most notable monument is the church of **Santo Spirito**, the church of a late 13th-century Cistercian convent whose nuns specialise in making and selling sweet almond and pistachio pastries. Ring the door bell marked '*monastero*' and say '*Vorrei dei dolci*' (I would like some pastries), and have plenty of euros ready (these are not charity cakes). The church is rather dilapidated but inside has fine Baroque stuccowork attributed to Giacomo Serpotta, while next door the restored remains of the Chiaramonte family's Norman palace now house the **Museo Civico di Santo Spirito**.

The **Cattedrale** on top of the hill incorporates Arab-Norman, Catalan Gothic and Baroque elements. The nave boasts an inlaid, coffered ceiling, while the graceful Baroque stuccowork in the choir contrasts with a severe Gothic chapel.

Ruins of the Temple of Olympian Zeus

WALK 8
Enna and Villa Romana

Explore the dramatically sited mountain city of Enna, then visit Piazza Armerina and Sicily's great Villa Romana, with the finest in-situ Roman floor mosaics in existence.

DISTANCE: 68km (42 miles)
TIME: A full day
START: Enna
END: Villa Romana
POINTS TO NOTE: Avoid crowds at the Villa Romana by arriving early in the morning, as the site opens.

Enna is the highest city in Sicily, lying 900m (3,000ft) above vast plains which once supplied the Greek and Roman empires with wheat. This former stronghold is an introspective city, often shrouded in mist – yet a welcome relief after the silent landscape that surrounds it. On the way to Villa Romana, stop briefly at the hill town of Piazza Armerina. Some of the town's late medieval palazzi and churches are crumbling but restoration is ongoing.

Enna

Enna ❶ is 85km (52 miles) west of Catania on autostrada A19, or 88km (55 miles) northeast of Agrigento on the winding SS640.

On a clear day there are fabulous views from Enna, and the best place to enjoy them is from the tallest tower, **Torre Pisano**, one of six surviving Norman and Swabian towers of the **Castello di Lombardia** (closed for restoration). You can park near the castle, then after your visit make your way down to **Via Roma**, the main street, which is flanked by dignified mansions and churches. The **Duomo** (Cathedral; free) was begun by Eleanor of Aragon in 1307 but rebuilt in a mixture of Gothic and Baroque styles. Enna's second medieval fortification is the isolated **Torre di Federico**, a tumbledown Swabian tower, on top of a hill towards Enna Bassa, the lower town.

After lunch in Enna, either at **Centrale**, see ①, or **Ariston**, see ②, take the SS561 from Enna Bassa, then join the SS117 bis. The steep switchback road takes you past Lago Pergusa, a lake encircled by a car-racing track, and then through a landscape of rough pastures and undulating wheatfields dotted with isolated farms.

Highly perched Enna

Aidone

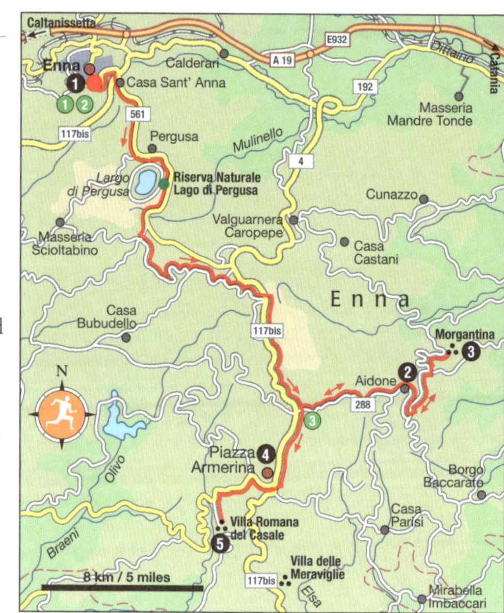

Shortly before Piazza Armerina, turn left onto the SS288, signed **Aidone** ❷. At the top of the old town is the **Museo Archeologico** (charge). Pride of place goes to the magnificent Greek statue **Venere di Morgantina**, a life-size Venus which was looted by tomb-robbers in the 1950s from the nearby Greek settlement of Morgantina. The statue mysteriously found its way to the Getty Museum in the States. After much wrangling, it was returned to Sicily in 2010, fully restored.

The site of **Morgantina** ❸, 4km/2.5 miles northeast of Aidone (charge) lies in beautiful quiet countryside with extensive Greek remains spreading over two hills. It is an atmospheric place – you may well have it to yourself in low season.

Piazza Armerina

The region's most renowned restaurant, **Al Fogher**, see ③, occupies an unlikely setting just after the SS117/SS288 junction about 3km (2 miles) before **Piazza Armerina** ❹. On arrival in the town, take the stairways and alleys up to the green-domed Baroque **Cattedrale** which crowns one hill and dominates the town. The church contains a venerated icon, the Madonna delle Vittorie, seen only during the Palio dei Normanniin August, an enactment of the taking of the town from the Saracens by Norman Count Roger in 1087. On the same square the sober 18th-century **Palazzo Trigona** has recently opened as the Museo della Città e del Territorio (charge), with multimedia installations enhancing its collections of ancient and medieval finds. Via Floresta beside the palace leads down to the

The town of Aidone

dilapidated Aragonese **Castello** (no access) and the faded palaces around it.

Villa Romana

From Piazza Armerina follow signs to **Villa Romana del Casale** ❺ (www.villaromanadelcasale.it; charge) nestling among thick woodland 5.5km (3.5 miles) away. Co-emperor Maximian, who ruled the waning Roman Empire with Diocletian, is said to have built this magnificent villa. It was later occupied by the Norman kings before disappearing under a landslide for 700 years. Excavations began in 1950 when a hoard of treasure was discovered.

Mosaics

The villa's key attraction lies in the exquisite and colourful Roman-African mosaics decorating the 40 rooms.

The entrance is via the *thermae* (baths). The centrepiece is the **Courtyard**, with a peristyle, pool and mosaic pairings of domestic and wild animals. The **Salone del Circo** (Circus Hall) has a vibrant depiction of a frenetic chariot race at the Circus Maximus in Rome. Off the courtyard, the **Room of the Cupid Fishermen** depicts a dolphin-riding mermaid admired by fishermen. Edging the main courtyard is the 60m/yd long **Corridor of the Great Hunt**, with superb mosaics of a sea separating Africa and Europe, and a swirling mass of movement with chariots, lions, cheetahs and rhinos. The **Room of Ten Maidens** presents the Villa's most famous mosaic of 'the Bikini Girls'. For dinner, your best option is to drive back to Al Fogher.

Food and drink

❶ Centrale

Piazza VI Dicembre 9, Enna; https://ristorantecentrale.net; €

This long-established restaurant in the heart of the town serves good, reasonably priced family fare such as tagliatelle with a *ragù* of rare breed pork and saffron-scented cheese. Benito Mussolini's signature is in the guestbook.

❷ Ariston

Via Roma 353, Enna; https://aristonenna.it; €€

A welcoming restaurant and Ennese institution, with hearty portions of traditional Sicilian fish and meat dishes. Good pizzas too (evenings only) and popular with the locals.

❸ Al Fogher

Viale Conte Ruggero (ex SS 117), Piazza Armerina; tel: 0935 684123; €€€

Outside the centre, this is an elegant high-end restaurant where you can expect artfully presented sophisticated and inventive gourmet dishes made with the freshest ingredients and a particularly interesting wine list.

Aidone archaeological museum artefacts

The famous 'Bikini Girls' mosaic

WALK 9
Siracusa

Alluring Siracusa is the summation of Sicilian splendour. The twin poles of attraction are the Greek archaeological park of Neapolis and seductive Ortigia, the island that is the city's cultural heart.

DISTANCE: 6km (3.75 miles) on foot; or 4km (2.5 miles) on foot and 2km (1.25 miles) by car, bus or taxi
TIME: A full day
START: Parco Archeologico della Neapolis
END: Ortigia
POINTS TO NOTE: The Parco Archeologico della Neapolis, where you can park, is 2km (1.25 miles) from the historic centre of Ortigia. Fairly frequent buses link the two. Parking in Ortigia is limited to residents, so use the multi-storey Parcheggio Talete, Via Veneto on its eastern coast.

Siracusa was one of the great powers of the ancient world, eventually surpassing Athens in prestige. The decisive battle was Siracusa's defeat of Athens at sea in 413 BC. Under Dionysius the Elder, the tyrant and monumental builder, the city had the grandest public works in the Western world. Archimedes, who was born here, was among its citizens. The Roman siege of Siracusa (213–211 BC) was marked by his ingenuity in devising mechanical devices to foil the enemy, including mirrors and magnifying lenses to blind them and perhaps even burn their boats. The Romans finally subdued the city in 211 BC, and in the 9th century it was destroyed by Arabs. As an early Christian centre, Siracusa was evangelised by St Peter and St Paul, and extensive catacombs served as both tombs and churches. It is on the island of Ortigia, a maze of splendid Baroque palazzi and churches, connected to the main town by two bridges, that you will likely spend most of your time.

Parco Archeologico della Neapolis

Northwest of the centre, the **Parco Archeologico della Neapolis** (Archaeological Park of Neapolis; https://parchiarcheologici.regione.sicilia.it/siracusa-eloro-villa-tellaro-akrai; charge) is the city's famed Classical park, set among firs and olives. It contains rough-hewn quarries, tombs and caverns, but the focus is the vast and grandiose Greek Theatre.

Siracusa harbour

Teatro Greco

Passing the rubble of **Ara di Ierone II** ❶, a huge sacrificial altar once decorated by telamones (stone giants), you get to the **Teatro Greco** ❷ (Greek Theatre). The open theatre, seating 15,000, is one of the largest and best-preserved in existence. It dates from 474 BC, though it was altered and added to by the Romans. Under the Greeks the theatre witnessed works by Sophocles, Euripides and Aeschylus, but during the Roman era it became an amphitheatre for gladiatorial combat. The theatre tradition is maintained today with Classical Greek dramas staged (in Italian) daily from the second week of May to early July (www.indafondazione.org).

Latomie

From the theatre a path leads down to the *latomie*, giant quarries which were used for the building of the ancient city, and more famously, as open-air prisons during the war with Athens (413 BC).

The **Orecchio di Dionisio** ❸ (Ear of Dionysius), a 47m (154ft) high arched cavern with remarkable acoustics, attracts almost as much tourist attention as the Greek Theatre. Carved into the rock and shaped like an upside-down ear lobe, it was supposedly employed by Dionysius to eavesdrop on his captives.

Beyond the cavern are the lemon scented quarries which were once used as a prison.

The adjoining **Grotta dei Cordari** (Ropemakers' Cave; closed indefinitely) is scored with chisel marks, because it was here that ropemakers stretched out their damp strands and tested their ropes for stress.

The largest of the quarries is the **Latomia del Paradiso** ❹, now a lush and colourful garden abounding in rocky arches, cacti, olive trees and citrus groves.

A separate entrance leads to the **Anfiteatro Romano** ❺ (Roman Amphitheatre), ringed by trees. Built in the 3rd century AD, it staged circuses and gladiatorial events. Exiting the park, take Via Augusto, then cross over the main road for Viale Teocrito.

Basilica and catacombs of San Giovanni

Other remnants of ancient Siracusa are scattered about the city. A much-visited site is the **Basilica of San Giovanni** ❻, signed to the left off Viale Teocrito. Formerly the cathedral of Siracusa, this is now a rather charming roofless ruin in a wild garden, but looks incongruous in its modern surrounds. Crooked steps lead down to the crypt of St Marcian, who was flogged to death in AD 254.

The **catacombe di San Giovanni** (San Giovanni Catacombs; www.kairos-web.com/luoghi/san-giovanni; charge, guided tours only) are an eerie network of catacombs, with thousands of empty niches

Teatro Greco

(looted by grave robbers) used until the 6th century. Fragments of frescoes and arcane symbols etched in the stone are still visible.

Museo Archeologico

Opposite the modern crinoline-domed **Madonna delle Lácrime**, built to house a statue of the Madonna which

Orecchio di Dionisio

reputedly wept for five days in 1953, the recently restored **Museo Archeologico Paolo Orsi** ❼ (Villa Landolina; https://parchiarcheologici.regione.sicilia.it/siracusa-eloro-villa-tellaro-akrai; charge) is Sicily's largest archaeological collection and one of the most important in Italy. It is divided into four sections: prehistory (A), Greek colonies in Sicily (B), sub-colonies and Hellenised centres (C) and Greek and Roman Siracusa (D). This is a huge and very confusing museum, with 18,000 pieces and long complex explanations (some in Italian only). To take it all in you would need several hours; alternatively, concentrate on the treasure trove of Classical statuary found in Siracusa. The prize piece is the headless and voluptuous **Venere Anadiomene** (Section D), also known as Venus Landolina because it was unearthed in the grounds of the Villa Landolina which houses the museum. There is also an Archaic fertility goddess suckling twins and a voracious Medusa with her tongue lolling out.

Ortigia

Avoid the dreary walk to Ortigia by taking a bus (101, 103, 104, 125 from Corso Gelone a ten-minute walk from the Archaeological Museum, tickets online at www.saisautolinee.it) or a taxi (rank opposite the Archaeological Park); otherwise drive to the Talete car park at Ortigia. Start your walk through this atmospheric and picturesque Island at the ruins of the **Tempio di Apollo** ❽ (565 BC), dedicated to the huntress Artemis (Diana) and her brother. If you are up for some local produce, stop first at Ortigia's lively market (Mon–Sat 8am–2pm), just steps away from the temple. This is also where some of Siracusa's most atmospheric restaurants are. Specialities include seafood, especially swordfish and shrimps, stuffed artichokes and *stimpirata di coniglio*, a rabbit and vegetable dish.

The centre

From the temple it is a short stroll up the shopping street, Corso Matteotti, to **Piazza Archimede** ❾. This grand Baroque stage set is framed by dignified mansions and focuses on a circular fountain of the river nymph Arethusa being transformed into a spring.
For good restaurants head for Via Gemmellaro, via the narrow Via Scinia off the main square. **Archimede**, see ①, serves excellent seafood and antipasti.

Piazza del Duomo

From Piazza Archimede, stroll south along the main **Via Roma**, then right for **Piazza del Duomo** ❿. The terrace of the **Grand Caffè del Duomo**, see ②, affords fine views. This is one of the most beautiful squares in Sicily, irregular in shape and flanked by a harmonious variety of Baroque buildings. Built over a temple to Athena, the **Duomo** ⓫ (Cathedral; free) is a summation of Sicilian history, with Byzantine apses, a Norman font, a medieval ceiling and

Museo Archeologico jars

Fontana di Diana

Boat cruises

If you need a break from walking, try a boat trip from Porto Grande: a short trip around Ortigia passes the medieval fortress of Castello Maniace, offering windswept views of the rocky Lungomare d'Ortigia. A more adventurous cruise is along the Fiume Ciane, a river 7km (4 miles) southwest of Siracusa off the SS115. The boat passes through groves of papyrus with cobweb-like tendrils and takes in the remains of the 6th-century Tempio di Giove Olimpico. Kiosks on the waterfront advertise tours or visit @labarcaortigia (on Instagram). Boat cruises only operate in season, normally from April to September.

Baroque facade and choir. Classical columns bulge through the external walls in Via Minerva, proof that the 5th-century BC temple was converted into a church in the 7th century AD. Cicero left a famous description of the sumptuous original decoration of the temple: walls painted with battle scenes and heroic portraits, doors of gold and ivory and a huge statue of the goddess Athena on the roof carrying a golden shield which flashed in the sun like a beacon for distant ships. Now the interior of the cathedral is impressively bare; the beamed roof, rough piers and patterned marble floor all reinforce the impression of a living Greek temple.

Among the fine palaces overlooking the piazza are the **Palazzo Municipale** (1629), the city council, north of the Duomo, and opposite the elegant **Palazzo Beneventano**, with a beautiful courtyard, which housed Nelson in 1789. South of the Duomo is the Palazzo Arcivescovile (Archbishop's Palace), with overhanging lemon trees and the late 17th-century church of **Santa Lucia alla Badia** ⓬. Ed: Painting not there any more. It is in the Basilica of Santa Lucia on the mainland, but adding this would involve creating a new map. It's not a lovely walk there from the other sites oin the mainland.

South of Piazza del Duomo

Beyond the piazza go down Via Picherali, then cross Piazza San Rocco and turn right for Via Capodieci. If staying for dinner, book a table at **Da Mariano**, see ③, on Vicolo Zuccolà just off Via Capodieci. Further on, **Palazzo Bellomo** is the loveliest Catalan Gothic mansion in Ortigia, and home to the **Galleria Regionale** ⓭ (charge). This is a collection of Sicilian 17th- and 18th-century paintings, the star of which is Antonello da Messina's *Annunciazione*.

The waterfront

Follow Via Capodieci to the seafront and the **Fonte Aretusa** ⓮, a freshwater spring venerated throughout the ancient world. Legend has it that the nymph Arethusa was fleeing the unwanted

Fonte Aretusa at night

attentions of the river god Alpheius. As the nymph reached Ortigia, the Olympian goddess Artemis (Diana) transformed her into a fountain, only for Alpheius to pull her under the waves and 'mingle his waters with hers'.

Originally a valuable source of water for the island, it was thought to be a resurgence of a river that disappeared underground at Olympia.

The tree-lined **Foro Italico** promenade runs north to **Porta Marina** ⓯, a gateway created in the 15th century as part of the Spanish fortifications, and beyond it **Porto Grande Marina**, where you could cool off with a fresh fruit drink or watermelon *granita* while watching excursion and fishing boats come and go.

The promenade running south from Fonte Aretusa is the **Lungomare Alfeo** ⓰, where you can join the evening *passeggiata* (stroll) or enjoy the sunset and sea views over an *aperitivo* in one of the many bars. Marking the end of the peninsula is **Castello Maniace** ⓱ (charge), built by Frederick II in 1239. The parade ground has become a popular place to stroll, picnic or hang out (there's a seasonal bar and plenty of benches), while in summer it becomes a concert venue. The entry fee gives access to the echoing halls, defensive ramparts and underground chambers (at their most evocative on stormy days when you can hear the waves crashing against the walls).

Food and drink

❶ Archimede

Via Gemellaro 8, Ortigia; tel: 0931 69701; €€

Something of an institution in Ortigia, Archimede has been going since 1938. Expect friendly service and a wide range of seafood pastas, half a dozen couscous dishes and a couple of meat options. Pizzas are also available, and there is a verandah.

❷ Gran Caffè del Duomo

Piazza del Duomo 18, Ortigia; €

The coffee and pastries are no different to those served anywhere else, but you can't beat this café for views of the Duomo and the square. If you crave something sweet and Sicilian, try their *cannoli* (pastry tube filled with sweet ricotta) or cool off with a gelato.

❸ Da Mariano

Vicolo Zuccolà 9, Ortigia; tel: 0931 67444; €

This is an authentic and long-established *osteria* with a welcoming atmosphere. Antipasti of ricotta and pistachio nuts, *salume* or marinated vegetables can be followed by rustic pastas or lamb, pork or rabbit from the Iblei mountains.

Diving in Ortigia

Thirteen-century Castello Maniace

TOUR 10
The Val Di Noto

Sicily's corner of Baroque splendour, currently the most dynamic region of the island, ideally calls for a couple of days' exploration. This tour takes in the finest of the towns: Noto, Modica, Scicli, Ragusa, and includes a picnic in the lush gorge of Cava d'Íspica.

DISTANCE: 110km (68 miles) from Siracusa
TIME: 2 days
START: Noto
END: Ragusa
POINTS TO NOTE: Modica makes a good base: it has some lovely hotels, B&Bs and restaurants. Alternatively consider Scicli or Ragusa.

The Val di Noto is currently the most dynamic part of Sicily. The Unesco-listed Baroque cities, built after the terrible earthquake of 1693, were designed to be theatrical and spectacular and have now been restored to their former glory. The churches and palaces are particularly fine seen after dark when the honey-coloured stone is lit up to magical effect.

If coming from Siracusa, take the A18, exit Noto, and head for the centre.

Noto

After the old **Noto Antica** was razed in the 1693 earthquake, Prince Landolina and Giuseppe Lanza (Duke of Camastra) lost no time in creating the new Noto on the flanks of a distant hill. Today it is the finest Baroque town in Sicily, with magnificently restored churches and palaces. On the lower slopes, three scenic squares unfold in a succession of dramatic perspectives, sculpted in golden stone.

Corso Vittorio Emanuele and Piazza Municipio

Arriving in the centre of **Noto** ❶, park alongside the **Giardini Pubblici** (Public Gardens) or behind the stadium and enter through the monumental **Porta Reale** gateway for the **Corso Vittorio Emanuele**. Conveniently, all of Noto's finest buildings are on or just off this pedestrianised main thoroughfare. On the right, at the top of a theatrical, grand flight of stairs, stands the church of **San Francesco** (free). Alongside it sits the old monastery of **San Salvatore**, and on the same piazza the richly decorated church of **Santa Chiara** (charge

Church of San Domenico, Noto

for tower). It's worth climbing the tower, up a steep spiral staircase, for the fabulous views at the top.

The Corso sweeps on to the majestic **Piazza Municipio**, on which stands the elegantly grand **Palazzo Ducezio** (charge), and facing it the splendid **Cattedrale di San Niccolò** (charge).

Palazzo Villadorata

Stop for coffee and pastries at **Caffè Sicilia**, see 1, across the road at No. 125, then take Via Corrado Nicolaci, almost opposite, where you will find the grandest mansion in town: the restored **Palazzo Nicolaci di Villadorata** (charge). This Baroque jewel has wonderful balconies decorated with friezes of griffins, mythical monsters, horses and cherubs. The interior is equally grand, with frescoed walls and ceilings.

Back on the Corso, continue on to **Piazza XVI Maggio**, graced by gardens of palms, monkey puzzle trees and a fountain of Hercules. Dominating is Gagliardi's masterpiece, the church of **San Domenico**, and facing it, the tiny and ornate **Teatro Comunale** (1850) (charge). Concerts are held here from October to May. If you are hungry, head downhill to the bustling **Trattoria del Carmine**, see 2.

Palazzo Nicolaci's elegant interior

Palazzo Nicolaci di Villadorata

Cava d'Íspica

From Noto take the SS 115 south, signed Ragusa and Rosolino. Just after Rosolino, take the inconspicuous turning on the right just after the Agip petrol station. Then follow signs for the **Cava d'Íspica** ❷ (www.cavadispica.org; charge), a 13km (8-mile) long limestone gorge which, with its catacombs and cave dwellings, makes a fascinating walk – even if you only do a short section. Just below the entrance is the **Catacomba Larderia**, early Christian catacombs, while close to the car park, the **Grotta di San Nicola** is a rock chapel with badly damaged late Byzantine frescoes, that was inhabited until the 1950s.

Modica

Perched on a ridge spilling down into a gorge, **Modica** ❸ is two towns in one: **Modica Alta** (high) and **Modica Bassa** (low). At first sight the setting is more prepossessing than the grey–brown town, but Modica repays exploration, from its mysterious alleys and mouth-watering food to its illutrious history as the most powerful fiefdom on the island. Although prosperous, it is an unpretentious sort of place, far from glitzy, even shabby in parts. On Easter Day, Sicilians don their Sunday best and flock to Modica for the festival of the Madonna Vasa Vasa. A statue of the Madonna in mourning, seeking her son, is paraded through the streets. When she meets the resurrected Christ her mantle changes from black to blue, doves fly out, bells peel and a jubilant crowd applauds the embrace (*vasa* vasa literally means 'kiss, kiss') of mother and son. This is one of the most moving and famous religious festivals in Sicily. Modica is also famous for its chocolate, which is sweet and slightly gritty.

Corso Umberto I

Follow signs to the centre and, once through the sprawling outskirts, you will arrive at **Corso Umberto** in Modica Bassa where you can usually find a parking space (tickets from *tabacchi*). This is the town's main street and it is flanked by the golden facades of palaces and churches, along with smart boutiques, wine bars and gourmet delights. A theatrical flight of steps, flanked by life-size statues of the 12 apostles, leads up to the opulent **Cattedrale di San Pietro** (free). Nearby, off Via Grimaldi, is the inconspicuous entrance to the ancient **Chiesa Rupestre di San Niccolò Inferiore** (charge), a grotto-like church, where three layers of frescoes dating from the 11th century were discovered in 1989.

Modica Alta

The pride of Modica is the **Duomo di San Giorgio** perched precariously above the alleys of historic Modica Alta and ideally approached by the 250-step staircase (you can also access it by road). A masterpiece by Gagliardi, the church boasts a sumptuous three-tiered

Cherubs on the church of Santa Chiara

Baroque facade and a soaring belfry, silhouetted against the sky. There are good views of Modica's rooftops from the terrace, but even better ones if you go higher to **San Giovanni Evangelista**, another grandiose Baroque church with a monumental flight of steps. At the end of Via Pizzo nearby, a belvedere known as **Il Pizzo** affords fine views over the town.

Alternatively join the locals in the *passeggiata* (evening stroll) along Corso Umberto I below, then dine at **Accursio**, see 3, just east of the Corso or **Fattoria delle Torri**, see 4, which is tucked away in an alley across the Corso from Piazza Matteoti.

Scicli

One of the smallest of the eight World Heritage towns, **Scicli** 4 is a Baroque gem, spilling along the bottom of a dramatic three-pronged limestone gorge. It came into its own as a tourist later than Noto and Ragusa – largely fuelled by its key role in the Montalbano TV series – and has an easy sophisticated charm. Via Mormino Penna is Scicli's showpiece, a scenographer's dream of a street, lined with exuberant and painstakingly restored Baroque churches and *palazzi*, including the Municipio fronted by the marvellous sculptural staircase that features in every episode of Montalbano, as the location of the police HQ. Other highlights include a filigree wrought- iron bandstand, a historic **pharmacy** (erratic opening times; charge) discovered a few years ago to have retained its stock, untouched, since it closed in the 1970s, and the church of **San Giovanni Evangelista** (free), which houses the astonishing Cristo di Burgos, a painting of Christ wearing what appears to be a white calf-length dirndl skirt (it is actually a shroud). Stop for a gourmet gelato at **Nivera**, see 5, or, if it is lunchtime, cut across to the little restaurant **Le Gioie**, see 6, overlooking the stone-paved dry riverbed that cuts through the town. Don't leave town without looking at

The Montalbano trail

On your travels through Ragusa province you are more than likely to see references to Montalbano, the detective in the popular TV series adapted from the detective novels by Antonio Camilleri and filmed in the region. The novels have become the best-read books to come out of Italy since *The Leopard*. Montalbano aficionados can follow the detective's footsteps and sit in his office in Scicli's Comune (Town Hall), which doubles as his office in the fictional town of Vigata. Scicli's churches and convoluted Baroque facades feature in most episodes of the series. So popular are the books and TV series in Italy there are Montalbano-themed holiday packages, as well as bus tours and train trips.

San Pietro painting, Modica

View of Modica

Palazzo Beneventano, whose balconies are embellished with fantastic corbels representing mythical beasts, Moors and ghoulish human masks. From here follow the signs up the hill that dominates the town, along an attractive winding path that leads up through a quarter of higgledy piggledly houses to the ruins of medieval fortifications. Near the top you will reach the partially restored remains of the church of **San Matteo** with great views down to the town. The adventurous could walk down via the overgrown track on the far side of the church, which winds up in what was once the town's poorest quarter, Chiafura, where until the late twentieth century, people were still living in cave-houses. Several have now been restored as quirky bijou homes.

Ragusa

Return towards Modica along the SP54, then follow the SS115 to **Ragusa** 5 (25.5km/16 miles). When Ragusa was reduced to rubble by the 1693 earthquake, the merchants built bland **Ragusa Alta** on the hill, but the aristocracy recreated **Ragusa Ibla** on the original valley site. The two merged as one town in 1926.

Ragusa Ibla

Ignore Ragusa Alta and follow the gorge crossed by three bridges to the Baroque city of Ragusa Ibla. Follow signs and leave the car in the large car park below **Piazza della Repubblica**. From here it is a 10-minute walk down to the centre of Ragusa Ibla. But first admire the stunning views of Ibla from **Santa Maria delle Scale** to the southwest. From this balcony over the town, the energetic can take the winding 250 steps down.

Ibla is an enchanting, timeless pocket of Sicily, where old-world charm and intimacy prevail. Gentrification has reversed the neglect in recent years; crumbling mansions are being restored, historic palaces have been converted to restaurants, bars and gourmet delis, and where once Ibla was deserted after dark, its pedestrianised quarter is now the focus for Ragusa's low-key nightlife.

Gagliardi's blue-domed **Cattedrale di San Giorgio** (free) is set high above **Piazza del Duomo**, the palm-lined cobbled piazza. The terraced cathedral is a masterpiece of graceful, swelling rhythms, embellished with decorative swirls and frills. Follow a visit to the cathedral with a stroll around the atmospheric Jewish ghetto, behind the church. Then if it's time for sustenance, head either to Michelin-star chef, Ciccio Sultano's **Il Duomo**, see 7, or for a more affordable and casual experience, one of the wonderful set lunches at his **Il Banchi**, see 8.

The main **Corso XXV Aprile**, on a hill, is lined by inviting eateries. Across the square at the end of the street, pause in the **Giardino Ibleo**, an exotic park with ruined churches. This is a popular spot for an evening stroll, with great views.

Cattedrale di San Giorgio

Food and drink

1 Caffè Sicilia

Corso Vittorio Emanuele 125, Noto; Tue–Sun 8am–11pm, closed Feb and two weeks in Mar; €

This is one of Sicily's most celebrated *pasticcerie*, dating from 1892, with home-made pastries, almond cakes, *granite*, *cassata* and ice creams.

2 Trattoria del Carmine

Via Ducezio 9; €€

Everything at this simple, family-run trattoria is fresh and homemade. Regional specialities include seafood-based pastas and *coniglio alla stimpirate*, a traditional Sicilian rabbit dish with a sweet and sour sauce.

3 Accursio

Via Clemente Grimaldi 41, Modica; www.accursioristorante.it/en; €€€

Chef Accursio Craparo's local Sicilian fare, using top quality ingredients and inspired by dishes that his mother used to make, has earned this elegant restaurant a Michelin star. Early booking recommended

4 Fattoria delle Torri

Vico Napolitano 14, Modica Alta; https://fattoriadelletorri.com; €€€

This charming *trattoria* serves wonderful traditional fare in a Baroque palatial setting.

5 Nivera

Via Mormino Penna 14, www.facebook.com/nivera.gelateria/?locale=it_IT; €

Gelateria creating fantastic ice creams, sorbets and granita from seasonal local ingredients – fig, ricotta, persimmon, prickly pear, cinnamon, almond, pistachio... you name it, they have ice-creamed it!

6 Le Gioie

Via Aleardi 5, 340 5479265; €€

Refreshingly simple little place run by a father and son, with tables overlooking the dry river that runs through the centre of town.

7 Il Duomo

Via Capitano Boccheri 31, Ragusa Ibla; www.cicciosultano.it; €€€€

Arguably the best restaurant in Sicily, the elegant Duomo is renowned for intense, elaborate reinterpretations of Sicilian cuisine.

8 I Banchi

Via Orfanotrofio 39; http://ibanchiragusa.it; €€

Styled as a "basilica of taste" by its creator, Ciccio Sultano of *Duomo*. At the root of it all is their fantastic home-made bread and pasta, along with meticulously sourced deli produce. Then there's café-style service for traditional (but exceptional) street food and pastries, and a more sophisticated set lunch.

View of Ragusa

Driving through Ragusa Ibla

WALK 11
Catania

Brave the industrial sprawl of Sicily's commercial powerhouse and discover a vibrant centre of bold Baroque buildings, boisterous food markets and lively streetlife.

DISTANCE: 4km (2.5 miles)
TIME: A half-day walk
START: Castello Ursino
END: Villa Bellini
POINTS TO NOTE: The market and some sites are closed on Sunday.

Catania lies in the shadow of brooding Mount Etna. In 1669 it unleashed a great torrent of lava that flowed over the city walls. Reconstruction was under way when the great earthquakes of 1693 swallowed up the city. Giovanni Battista Vaccarini, a Palermitan architect influenced by grand Roman Baroque, rebuilt the entire city, using the sombre black lava stone.

Castello Ursino

Start at Piazza Federico II di Svevia, dominated by the 13th-century **Castello Ursino** ❶, former fortress of Frederick II and a rare surviving pre-earthquake vestige. The fortress overlooked the Ionian Sea before Etna's lava flow pushed the coastline a quarter of a mile seawards. It now houses the **Museo Civico** (Civic Museum; https://museocivicocastelloursino.comune.catania.it; charge).

Head north from the piazza, turn right into Via Transito and follow your nose (literally) for the Fish Market.

Fish Market

At the raucous **Pescheria** ❷ (Fish Market; Mon–Sat 8am–2pm), sea bream, swordfish, sea urchins, squirming eels and lobsters are laid out together with meat carcasses, sheep's heads, fruit, veg and herbs. **Osteria Antica Marina**, see ①, is renowned for fish (book ahead).

Piazza del Duomo

Take the steps up by the fountains to **Piazza del Duomo** ❸, the Baroque centrepiece of the city. In the centre Vaccarini's delightful **Fontana dell'Elefante** is the city symbol. Rebuilt after the earthquake, the Baroque **Duomo** (Cathedral; free) houses the tombs of Aragonese royals and of the composer Bellini.

The cathedral

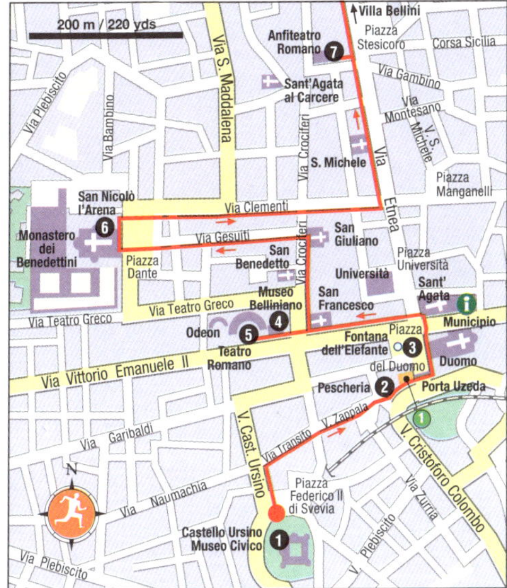

Via Vittorio Emanuele II

On Piazza San Francesco, the **Museo Belliniano** ❹ (charge) was the birthplace of the composer Bellini in 1801 and houses his death mask and opera scores. The **Teatro Romano** ❺ (charge) was the venue for battles between exotic beasts and gladiators.

Via Crociferi and San Nicolò l'Arena

From Piazza San Francesco go north along **Via Crociferi** lined with lofty 18th-century Baroque churches, convents and palazzi. Turn left at Via Gesuiti for **San Nicolò l'Arena** ❻ perhaps the largest and eeriest church in Sicily. Work was curtailed by the 1693 earthquake and the church was later abandoned, incomplete. The huge adjoining Benedictine monastery is now part of the university. Hourly guided visits can be booked via the website www.monasterodeibenedettini.it; charge). All tours include the magnificent cloisters and a hanging garden.

From Piazza Dante head east to **Via Etnea**, the main shopping street. Going north, towards Etna, cross **Piazza Stesicoro**, with its **Anfiteatro Romano** ❼, the remains of the largest amphitheatre in Sicily. Carry on to **Villa Bellini**, delightful gardens where you can retreat from the bustle.

Food and drink

① Osteria Antica Marina

Via Pardo 29; www.anticamarina.it; €€

This osteria is in the heart of the Fish Market, so the fish couldn't be fresher. Choose from fish antipasti, pasta dishes with seafood and grilled fish.

Catania fish market

Fontana dell'Elefante statue

WALK 12
Taormina

Taormina is Sicily's glitziest and most dramatically situated resort, perched on a hill overlooking the coast and Mount Etna. Stroll through the centre, soaking up the views, or hike up the hill to Castelmola. An opera, ballet, film or rock concert at the Teatro Greco makes a memorable end to the day (for programme see www.vaitaormina.com/eventi).

DISTANCE: Walk in Taormina, 3km (2 miles), optional 2km (1.25-mile) walk to Castelmola
TIME: A half-day walk
START/END: Corso Umberto I. Optional excursions to Mazzarò, Isola Bella and Castelmola
POINTS TO NOTE: Cars should be left in hotel car parks, or in one of the town's three car parks. Lumbi Parking on the approach road has a shuttle service to the centre ; Mazzarò, on the coast road, is linked to the centre by funivia; and Porta Catania is in easy walking distance of the centre. A scenic rail route runs along the coast to Taormina's Giardini station, with a 10-minute bus ride to the top of the town. To avoid the worst of the crowds, see the Teatro Greco at 9am or at the end of the day.

It is no surprise that the Greeks and Romans took advantage of the perfect setting on the east of the island and built a theatre here. Taormina is the royal box in one of the grandest of nature's theatres. The resort stands perched on the lower of a descending series of crags nearly 300m (1,000ft) above the coast. There are spectacular views in all directions, by day and night: to the south Mount Etna looms, to the north there are views across sweeping bays and the dark hills of Calabria.

Taormina makes an enticing base for excursions – though midsummer is best avoided. Spring is a lovely time to visit, given the mild weather and profusion of pink blossom. But don't expect empty streets – the town lives off tourism and from early spring to late autumn it's abuzz with visitors.

The centre comprises a main street and a maze of steep, narrow alleys, mostly reserved for pedestrians. It is still very charming in a restored and stagey way, with colourful window boxes, lemon and orange groves, and charming alfresco cafés on small squares.

The Teatro Greco with mighty Mount Etna in the background

The Centre

Most visitors enter Taormina at **Porta Messina** ❶, the gateway leading into the pedestrianised **Corso Umberto I**, the normally packed thoroughfare that bisects the town. The town's palazzi have been converted into big-name designer emporia, craft shops, boutiques, jewellers and bars, while luxury delis display bottled peppers, candied fruit and a mind-boggling range of pesto and condiments. Side streets reveal balconies hung with geraniums and bougainvillaea.

Palazzo Corvaja

At the east end of the Corso on Piazza Vittorio Emanuele II, the tourist office occupies **Palazzo Corvaja** ❷, a historic mansion with a crenellated Arab tower. In the chamber on the first floor the Sicilian 'Parliament' met in 1411, now it is home to folkloric exhibits of the **Museo Siciliano di Arte e Tradizioni Populari** (Sicilian Museum of Art and Popular Traditions) including 120cm (47in) -high Catanian marionettes based on historical figures. From here, walk uphill to the **Odeon Romano** ❸, a Roman concert auditorium almost concealed by the charming church of **Santa Caterina**.

The Greek Theatre

From here follow the flow along the gentle slope of Via Teatro Greco to Taormina's most famous site, the **Teatro Greco** ❹ (https://parconaxostaormina.com; charge). The setting, overlooking smouldering Etna, the coast and Calabrian mountains, is pure drama. The theatre was carved out of the hillside by the Greeks in the 3rd century BC and was later enlarged by the Romans. While in Greek theatres sea and sky were the natural backdrop, the Romans preferred proscenium arches. They added a double portico and colonnades behind the stage, closing off views of sea and mountains. The attention of spectators was instead focused on the arena, which under the Romans became a circus exclusively for gladiatorial combat. Today the theatre makes a magnificent

Busy Piazza Aprile

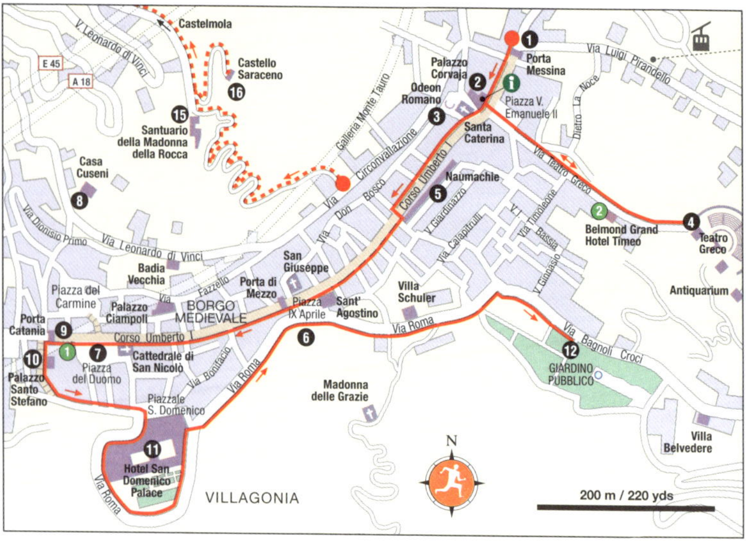

setting for opera, drama, ballet, music and cinema (from June to September).

Naumachie and Piazza IX Aprile

From theatrical heights walk back down Via Teatro Greco and pause for a drink in the busy piazza before re-entering the fray on Corso Umberto I. The first passageway on the left leads to the **Naumachie** ❺, a hybrid construction which began as a vaulted cistern connected to the city baths but became a Greek nymphaeum (a monument consecrated to nymphs) and Roman gymnasium. The ancient arched buttress walls remain, propping up the Corso.

Piazza IX Aprile ❻, halfway down the Corso, has panoramic views of Etna and the sea. **Sant'Agostino**, the austere 15th-century church on the square, has been converted into a cosy library, while the 17th-century **San Giuseppe** has an ornate rococo stucco interior. Continue along the Corso, passing beneath the **Porta di Mezzo**, or clock-tower, into the **Borgo Medievale**, the oldest quarter of the town.

Piazza del Duomo

Piazza del Duomo ❼ is a popular meeting place and home to the crenellated **Cattedrale di San Nicolò**. **Vecchia Taormina**, see ➊, is a good spot for lunch. From the square,

Concert at the Teatro Greco

stepped alleys lead up to Piazza del Carmine and the **Badia Vecchia** ❽, a battlemented 15th-century abbey. Opposite Casa Cuseni (www.casacuseni.it), the Bohemian home of Daphne Phelps, author of *A House in Sicily*, can be explored if you book in advance. The Corso ends at **Porta Catania** ❾, the archway that matches the Porta Messina gate.

Down the steps, off Piazza Sant'Antonio, the **Palazzo Santo Stefano** ❿ is a gracious ducal palace with a concoction of Norman windows, lava-stone cornices and a lacy frieze of delicate wood inlay – an Arab legacy. From here the road leads to **San Domenico** ⓫, a 15th-century monastery, and now a Four Seasons hotel, as well as the location for the hit HBO TV series *The White Lotus*.

Giardino Pubblico

Stroll back along the winding Via Roma, which brings you to the exotic **Giardino Pubblico** ⓬ (also called Villa Comunale; daily dawn–dusk; free). The hanging gardens, dotted with pagoda-style follies, tropical plants and with a sea-view terrace, were the creation of Florence Trevelyan, an eccentric Scots aristocrat who had to leave Britain after an affair with the Prince of Wales, the future Edward VII.

Taormina by night

A stroll after dark through the centre of Taormina is an essential experience. The Catalan Gothic facades are eerily illuminated, the squares tinged pink in the moonlight. The main form of evening entertainment is the *passeggiata* along Corso Umberto I – the shops close only when

Catering for all

Taormina was first publicised by a trio of Germans: a writer, a painter and a photographer. In 1787 the writer Goethe pronounced Taormina 'a patch of paradise on earth'. The artist Otto Geleng later drew visitors to the island with his romantic landscapes. Von Gleden spent 50 years from 1880 photographing nude shepherd boys, emulating bucolic poems. Draped in exotic leopard skins, Taormina's lithe peasants scandalised Sicilian society and made Taormina a gay mecca.

This louche image runs in parallel with Taormina's reputation as Sicily's earliest, smartest winter resort. A 'fashionable loafing place', it was patronised by leisured Edwardians, including Daphne Phelps uncle, Robert Kitson, who bought and restored Casa Cuseni. D.H. Lawrence had a villa here in the early 1920s, and during the 1940s such luminaries as Gloria Vanderbilt, Marlene Dietrich, Rita Hayworth and Joan Crawford were part of the social scene. The terraced town still attracts a chic crowd and remains Sicily's most gay-friendly resort.

Painter on Piazza Aprile

Villa Comunale di Taormina

Food and drink

1 Vecchia Taormina
Vico Ebrei 3; www.vecchiataormina.it; €
Popular pizzeria in the heart of town with a wood-burning oven and courtyard seating.

2 Belmond Grand Hotel Timeo Restaurant
Via Teatro Greco 40; www.belmond.com/grand-hotel-timeo-taormina; €€€€
Fine dining framed by a timeless panorama in which Etna and Capo Taormina are the stars. To make the most of the views, come for a light lunch, or at cocktail hour for a chic drink accompanied by the spectacle of sunset over the bay.

3 Antico Caffè San Giorgio
Piazza S. Antonio, Castelmola; €
Follow in the footsteps of Churchill, Rockefeller and Pope John Paul II (to name a few), and sip a sweet almond wine on the terrace as you soak up stupendous views of Taormina and the Gulf of Naxos. Rustic antipasti and *granite* are also on offer.

everyone goes home. Drive down to Giardini-Naxos for affordable seafood. Or head to **Belmond Grand Hotel Timeo Restaurant**, see 2 for something a little fancier.

Mazzarò and Bella Isola

Unless it's peak season, consider an afternoon on the pebbly, well-equipped beaches of **Mazzarò** 13, situated below Taormina. The cable car (charge) from Via Luigi Pirandello runs every 15 minutes.

Take a rowing boat beyond the Capo Sant'Andrea for the lovely cove with two beaches (also accessible on foot) and the tiny **Isola Bella** 14, which has become a marine reserve, popular with divers and sunbathers. The 'Roman Temple' shipwreck dive, 26m (85ft) down, reveals marble columns which were destined for a temple in Taormina.

Castelmola

If a hike up the hill appeals, take the path to the **Santuario della Madonna della Rocca** 15 above Taormina, and just above it the ruins of the **Castello Saraceno** 16. The walk starts at Via Circonvallazione in Taormina, with a steep path signed 'Castel Taormina/Madonna della Rocca'.

Have a cooling drink at the Castello Saraceno, admire the views and, if it's not too hot, carry on up to **Castelmola** 17 (around 50 minutes), a hamlet with a ruined castle perched on a limestone peak.

Castelmola is quite touristy but worth the climb for the panorama. Try a glass of *vino alla mandorla* (almond wine), the sweet local tipple. **Antico Caffè San Giorgio**, see 3, in the square, has the finest views.

View up to Castelmola

TOUR 13

Exploring Etna: Foothills and Ascent

Start at the stunning Alcantara Gorge, skirt the volcanic foothills of Mount Etna and visit black lava villages in the jaws of the volcano. Add another day or half-day for the ascent to the main crater.

DISTANCE: 187km/116 miles (137km/85.5 miles if returning to Catania)
TIME: Foothills drive: one day; ascent: half or one day
START: Taormina
END: Catania or Taormina
POINTS TO NOTE: Choose a clear day for views of Etna. Take swimming gear and sturdy shoes for the Alcantara Gorge. If climbing Etna you will need warm clothes – even in summer – walking shoes or boots, hat, sunglasses, sunscreen and water. Jacket and boots can be rented. Independent hikers should take advice before setting off. For trekking companies with professional local guides contact Etna Experience (www.etnaexperience.com) or Guide Etna Nord (www.guidetnanord.com). Climbs to the crater are subject to weather conditions and volcanic activity and can be cancelled without warning. Tour agencies in Catania and on Etna offer half- or full-day 4-wheel-drive and trekking excursions.

Etna is Europe's largest and most active volcano, and it makes its presence felt. Whether snow-capped, charcoal-coloured or partially swathed in mist, it is visible from afar. *Mongibello*, the local name for Etna, comes from the Arabic for mountain. The native Siculi tribes believed that Adranus, the god of fire, fashioned the volcano, while to the Greeks, Etna was Vulcan's forge, moulding black magic from incandescent magma. To modern Sicilians, Mongibello is sacred, beneficent yet pitiless, the gold of fertility and the god of destruction. 'Etna has taken back my orchard!' cried a farmer in 1992, as a tide of molten lava engulfed his land.

An eruption in 693 BC reached the coast, while the 1669 explosion wiped out Catania, after which the lava took eight years to cool. The 21st century has seen a flurry of seismic activity. In 2002 it destroyed the ski lifts, cable car and tourist complex at the Rifugio Sapienza southern gateway, and intense eruptions have continued sporadically ever since. Notwithstanding, over 20 percent of Sicilians still choose

Mighty Etna

to live on these risky slopes.

On clear days the views are stupendous. In winter (and often until late April or May) Etna is snow-capped. At the lower levels, the potassium- and phosphate-rich soil is ideal for citrus groves, above them vines and olives flourish, then higher up broom and prickly pears give way to pine groves. Above the tree line lies a moonscape scarred by clinker.

The Alcantara Gorge

From Taormina drive south to Giardini-Naxos and take the SS185 inland. After 15km (9 miles), visit the popular **Gole dell'Alcantara** ❶ (www.golealcantara.it; charge for lift), a stunning 20m (66ft) deep gorge. The pitted river canyon was created by the collision of volcanic magma and the cooling water of the river, the impact throwing up lavic prisms in warped shapes. A lift leads down to the grey-green river and the so-called beach, where in summer you can paddle in the icy waters or hire waders and wetsuits to explore further. Beyond are rapids that can be explored on guided rafting, kayaking and canyoning (details on the website).

Castiglione di Sicilia

Beyond the gorge, **Francavilla di Sicilia** ❷ is set in a fertile valley of citrus plantations, with King Roger's ruined castle occupying a lone mound. Follow signs up to **Castiglione di Sicilia** ❸, an atmospheric village perched on a crag. It retains some Greek ramparts but is essentially a bastion of basalt churches and quiet, medieval alleys. The ruined **Norman Castle** dominates the valley, with lovely views over red-tiled roofs to citrus groves beyond. Pop into the Caseificio Alcantara Formaggi on Via Federico II to buy fresh ricotta for a picnic or seasoned cheeses to take home (www.alcantaraformaggi.it).

Randazzo

Enjoy the views of Etna as you wind south to join the SS120. Turn right here for **Randazzo** ❹, the best preserved medieval town on the northern slopes of Etna. During Swabian times this was a cool summer retreat for the royal court. Although lying in the jaws of Etna, the town survived numerous eruptions, but as the Nazis' last stand in Sicily, suffered from Allied bombs. What remains is a tribute to the medieval rivalry between Randazzo's three communities: Latins, Greeks and Lombards settled in different parishes, and each of their crenellated churches became the cathedral for a three-year term. The Catholics triumphed, and **Santa Maria** on **Via Umberto I** is now the cathedral. This main street contains the severe Swabian summer palace and other symbols of Randazzo's past role as a royal city. At the far end the **Chiesa San Martino** is graced by a 13th-century banded lava and limestone bell tower, matched by a grey and white stone Baroque

Gole dell'Alcantara

facade. Close by is the **Castello Svevo**, a medieval castle and Bourbon prison, now the **Polo Museale Civico** (charge), with archaeological finds and Sicilian puppets.

Follow one of the alleys to the city walls and views of ruined battlements beyond, then consider lunch at **San Giorgio e Il Drago**, see 1, a rustic-style restaurant near the church

Randazzo

Alcantara blooms

of Santa Maria, or the **Trattoria Veneziano**, see ❷, 2km (1.25 miles) out of town, off the SS120 going east.

Castello Nelson

Continue on the circular route, branching left onto the S284 south of Randazzo. **Maletto** ❺ further south, famous for its strawberries, offers views of recent lava flows. From here follow signs for **Maniace** and **Castello Nelson** ❻ (https://castellonelsondibronte.it; charge).

Founded by Count Roger, this is best-known as the one-time estate of Admiral Horatio Nelson. It was presented to him by Ferdinand IV when he was created Duke of Bronte in 1799. Nelson's descendants lived here until 1981 and, although the estate was broken up, Nelson memorabilia remains, from paintings of sea battles to the admiral's port decanter. The Benedictine abbey was destroyed by the 1693 earthquake but retains the late Norman chapel with original wooden ceiling and a portal with fine carvings. Don't expect a castle – it's more like an English manor house.

Bronte

Follow signs for **Bronte** ❼, taking you onto the SS120 and SP165. The road winds through walnut and chestnut groves, then, nearing Bronte, plantations of pistachio trees. These produce 80 percent of Italy's crop. The pistachios, harvested biannually, are used in pasta dishes, patisserie and ice creams, and a pistachio festival takes place annually in the first 10 days of October. Pistachios apart, Bronte is unremarkable: a rather shabby town sandwiched between two lava flows.

Adrano

Bronte gives way to alpine plains, scrubland and lava-encrusted slopes – relics of the 1985 eruption. The SS284 takes you south to **Adrano** ❽. Set on Etna's southwest slopes, this market town was once the Greek city of Adranon, and was celebrated for its sanctuary to Adranus, the Siculi god of fire. Its outskirts are dotted with Greek masonry, matched by sections of city wall beyond Via Buglio. The town's battered charm lies in the busy **Piazza Umberto** with the massive **Norman Castle**, rebuilt by Roger I and the Aragonese, and the neighbouring **Chiesa Madre**, a much-restored church of Norman origin incorporating basalt columns from an ancient Greek temple.

Unless you are hiking from Nicolosi or taking the cable car from Rifugio Sapienza, follow the SS284 Catania road from Adrano which feeds into the autostrada. From here it is only half an hour's drive back to Taormina along the fast A18, allowing perhaps time for a sunset cocktail overlooking Etna's fireworks.

Ascent of Etna

Be advised by the experts because, depending on volcanic activity,

The town of Bronte

Etna can be a damp squib or the most dramatic memory of your stay. Without a guide, suitably clad hikers can clamber about at their own risk up to a certain altitude, currently around 3,000m (9850ft), 323m (1060ft) short of Etna's height. The two principal approaches are Etna Nord (north) and Etna Sud (south).

Southern approach – Rifugio Sapienza

The simplest way of seeing the crater is the cable-car excursion from **Rifugio Sapienza** ❾ (at 1920m/6,300ft), which also includes an optional guided drive and walk to the summit. From Taormina it is a 60km (37.5-mile) drive: take the A18 autostrada, exit at Giarre and head west via Santa Venerina and Zafferana Etna. Alternatively there is a bus (Mon–Sat) departing from Catania's Stazione Centrale at 8.15am and returning at 4.30pm, and an extra one at 11am in August. The Rifugio has a live TV feed from the top, showing the conditions, so you can check before departing. The **cable car** (www.funiviaetna.com; Apr–Nov 9am–4.15pm, Dec–Mar 9am–3.45pm; charge), used by skiers in winter, takes you to **La Montagnola** ❿ (2,640m/8,200ft), where you can stop for a basic coffee and admire the views. From here there is the option of a 4-wheel-drive minibus tour of the craters with guide (Mar–Nov; charge) to **Torre del Filósofo** ⓫ at 2,920m.

Volcano railway

The alternative to a car tour is the quaint Circumetnea Railway (www.circumetnea.it) which skirts the lower slopes of Etna. This single-track rail route, which has been in existence since 1894, is a leisurely 114km (71-mile) journey, starting in Catania, taking in Adrano, Bronte and Randazzo and returning to the coast at Giarre-Riposto south of Taormina.

This is a wonderful trip and excellent value, affording fine views of the fertile lower slopes as well as Etna itself. Depending on the timetable and sections open you will have time to stop off at one of the stations. Get up early and make sure you have a timetable. Randazzo is the most appealing town en route.

By foot

The energetic can go all the way up from the Rifugio Sapienza by foot. It takes around four hours to get up – faster, of course, coming down. Less challenging is the cable car and walking the rest of the way (around 2km/1.25 miles). For other guided mountain treks from the south, visit www.etnaguide.com.

Northern approach – Piano Provenzana

The gateway to Etna's northern slopes is **Piano Provenzana**, a ski resort 16km (10 miles) southwest

Street view of Adrano

Rifugio Sapienza

Food and drink

1 San Giorgio e Il Drago
Piazza San Giorgio 28, Randazzo; www.ristorantesangiorgioeildrago.it; €€
The good-value St George and the Dragon offers freshly-made pasta with funghi or wild herbs from Etna, followed by meaty regional mains such as rabbit with caper and olive sauce.

2 Trattoria Veneziano
Km 187 SS120, Contrada Arena, Randazzo; www.ristoranteveneziano.it; €€
Just out of town, this is a modern restaurant with pretensions, but it has tasty regional dishes. Mushrooms from the slopes of Etna are a speciality. Try them with rigatoni pasta or with rabbit or wild boar.

3 Rifugio Ragabo
Strada Mareneve, Pineta Bosco Ragabo, Linguaglossa; http://ragabo.it; €
Cosy and warm, this Alpine-style *rifugio*, 1450m above sea level, has a restaurant where you can keep the cold at bay with hearty mountain fare, including home-made pasta. There is also simple accommodation, and they organise excursions.

of **Linguaglossa** 12. There is no public transport, so you will need to drive. (From Taormina exit the A18 autostrada at Fiumefreddo and follow SS120 towards Randazzo for Linguaglossa. From there follow the mountain road to Piano Provenzana, passing the **Rifugio Ragabo**, see 3, where you could stop for lunch. The climb on foot is a 6–7 hour round trip (contact www.guidetnanord.com). If you prefer the idea of a lovely drive, from Piano Provenzana follow signs to Rifugio Citelli. The views are tremendous, stretching from the Nebrodi mountains to Taormina, and over the sea to Calabria.

What to see

While it would be foolish to expect apocalyptic eruptions and a river of molten lava, Etna is fascinating in its many moods and offers plenty to see, from the purplish-brown heaps of volcanic rubble to the comical decapitated cones and gaping lava mouths. Around the cones, the encrusted lava is black, mauve, grey or red, depending on age. If you're lucky you may see a glowing red crater, the belching of sulphurous vapours, a shower of sparks or gaseous explosions.

Etna's eruptive mode shows little sign of abating. The glittering red cone is visible from Catania during the day, while visitors in Taormina are virtually guaranteed a nightly spectacle of molten bombs shooting from Etna's cones.

Descending Etna

TOUR 14
The Aeolian Islands

Shaped by wind and fire, these tiny volcanic islands rise up from indigo seas off Sicily's north coast. Though popular with visitors in summer, in low season the archipelago still offers a real sense of adventure. Base yourself in Lípari for two to three days and ferry-hop to explore the smaller islands.

DISTANCE: From Milazzo to Lípari, then to the other islands: 356 km (221 miles)
TIME: 3 days
START: Milazzo
END: Lípari
POINTS TO NOTE: For information on how to get to the islands, see page 132. Cars are not allowed access in summer unless you are staying for at least a week, but vehicles can be left in private garages in Milazzo. If you only have a day to spare, consider a Panarea and Strómboli excursion (www.minicrociereisoleeolie.com), leaving Milazzo at noon, returning at 11pm, enabling you to watch Stromboli erupt at night. If climbing the Gran Cratere on Vulcano, take water, stout shoes, hat and sunscreen. For Stromboli hiking boots and clothes can be rented on the island.

The Greeks named the islands after Aeolus, the hospitable god of the winds who lived on Lípari and gave Ulysses a wineskin of winds to guide his ship back home to the Greek island of Ithaca. But even Aeolus, assuming he was more than a myth, is recent compared to the first settlers who arrived in Lípari in the 5th millennium BC. Prior to their arrival a volcano on Lípari had erupted, spewing huge quantities of magma which solidified to become obsidian. The hard black volcanic glass was much prized for crafting sharp tools and the island grew prosperous by trading them in the Mediterranean.

The islands were regarded as remote and inhospitable until around 50 years ago. Today these Unesco World Heritage dots in the Tyrrhenian Sea are inundated from mid-July to the end of August, but they are a delight in spring, early summer and autumn. Winter, when boats are often cancelled and you can get stranded on the islands, is best avoided.

Lípari (36 sq km/14 sq miles) is the largest and the hub of the archipelago. With its choice of accommodation, excursions and water sports, this makes the best base. The tours below take you

View over the Aeolian Islands from Vulcano

to smouldering Vulcano, spectacular Strómboli, chic Panarea and laidback Salina, but if staying longer you might also consider seeing Filicudi and Alicudi, remote rocky outcrops at the western end of the archipelago, with wild unspoilt scenery.

Lípari

Hydrofoils from Milazzo take around an hour and most stop at Vulcano en route. Ferries and hydrofoils dock at Marina Lunga, the bustling main port of **Lípari** ❶. From here take the café- and shop-lined **Corso Vittorio Emanuele**, where the *passeggiata* seems to take place most of the day. Tiny *vici* or alleys, crammed with potted plants and Vespas, lead up from this main *corso*, linking with the only other main road, the Via Garibaldi. Lípari town is the main attraction of the island, but away from the town there are mountains to climb, hot springs and bright white hillsides and beaches of pumice. Cars, scooters or bikes can be hired, or there are public buses that do a full circuit of the island from June to September. The coast, with its multicoloured cliffs, clear indigo waters, caves and grottoes is best explored on a boat excursion.

The Citadel

From Via Garibaldi the **Via Concordato**, a wide cobbled stairway, leads up to the splendid **Citadel** Ⓐ, built by the Spanish in the 16th century and absorbing a Greek tower and walls from the 4th century BC. The Norman cathedral was burnt down by Barbarossa in 1544 and the church you see today, the **Cattedrale di San Bartolomeo**, crowning the Citadel, is largely Baroque, but retains Norman vaults and cloister.

Archaeological Museum

Over the centuries, volcanic ash, spread by the Mediterranean mistral, formed 9m (29.5ft) strata on the citadel. A huge, painstaking excavation in the 1950s–70s yielded evidence of continuous occupation from the 4th millennium BC. The outstanding **Museo Archeologico Regionale Eoliano** Ⓑ (https://parchiarcheologici.regione.sicilia.it/isole-eolie/biglietti/museo-luigi-bernabo-brea-lipari; charge), in buildings either side of the cathedral, holds a treasure trove of prehistoric and classical artefacts found on Lípari and other parts of southern Italy.

The former Bishop's Palace houses the Neolithic and Bronze Age exhibits, including many tools crafted in obsidian. The Classical section displays burial urns, decorated vases and an extraordinary rich collection of 100 terracotta theatrical masks discovered in tombs from the 4th to 3rd century BC.

Marina Corta

Via Garibaldi drops down to **Marina Corta**, a colourful and busy little port, with small boats coming and going. Survey the scene from an alfresco table or have a leisurely

Lípari harbour

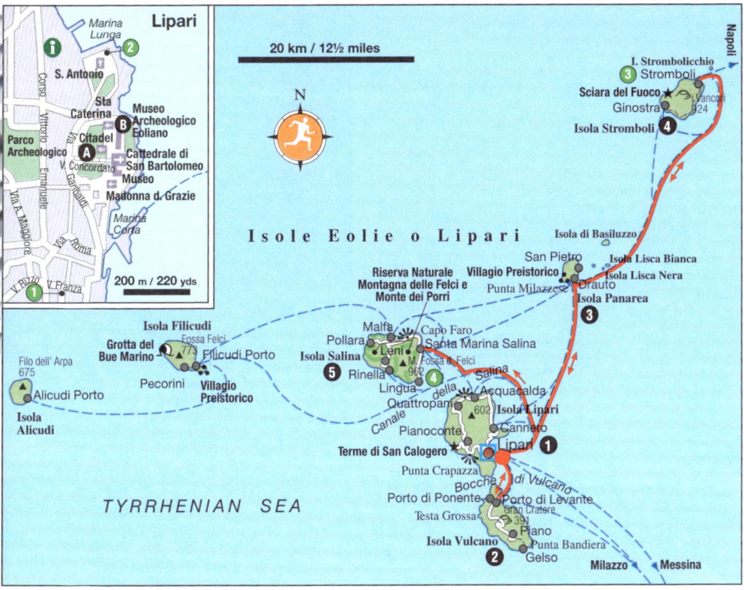

typically Aeolian lunch in a lovely setting at nearby **La Nassa**, see ①.

Vulcano

Vulcano ② is home of the god of fire. Excursion boats depart regularly from Marina Corta on Lípari (try bargaining off season), fishermen offer scenic trips in summer or hydrofoils/ ferries depart from Marina Lunga.

On arrival you're greeted by sulphurous odours coming from the smouldering **Gran Cratere**. In recent years the emissions from Vulcano have caused increasing concern, but the volcano is closely monitored, and if there is any danger at all, residents are evacuated and tourists banned. If the volcano is calm, the hour's hike up (charge for the path) is not too challenging but can be very hot. Allow time for walking around the peak and admiring the dramatic views.

The volcano supplies the island with its other main activity: thermal mud baths, said to cure skin disorders and rheumatic pains. Below the crater you can wallow in the warm *fanghi* (charge), shallow pools of thick mud, then clean up in the thermally

Mud bath on Vulcano

heated seawater pool, or head on to **Spiaggia Sabbia Nera**, a big sweep of black volcanic beach with red-hot sand where you can take a refreshing dip and admire the sunset.

Back on Lípari, try **Il Filippino**, see 2, in the upper town.

Panarea and Strómboli

Combine the islands of **Panarea** 3 and **Strómboli** 4 on a day trip, staying to watch the sunset and the volcano explosions. An excursion which costs little more than the hydrofoil is the simplest option. Hydrofoil and ferry services are limited, especially off season when you cannot see both islands and be back in Lípari in a day.

Fashionable little Panarea is the prettiest of the Aeolian Islands, with its dazzling white cubed houses, spectacular formations of volcanic rock and divinely clear waters. Wealthy Italians from the north have villas here and international celebrities visit in the summer. Apart from people-watching you can swim in the aquamarine waters of Cala Junca, visit the Neolithic village at Punta Milazzase and take boat trips to offshore islets.

Strómboli

Fiery Strómboli is the most theatrical of the islands: a volcanic cone rising out of the sea, whose crater emits a constant stream of magma. Occasional evacuations still happen, but the last serious eruption was in April 2003, when rocks fell onto the rooftops in the village of Ginostra, and triggered a tsunami. The island was put on the tourist map in 1949 when Ingrid Bergman and Roberto Rossellini starred in the film *Strómboli*.

Most excursions are planned so you can watch the pyrotechnics from the sea at night. Boats stop near the dramatic **Sciara del Fuoco**, the fiery slope where lava from the craters flows down to the sea. More challenging is the ascent up 924m (3,000ft) with a volcanologist in the early evening, arriving before sunset. It's a tough three plus hours up, then about two back down (for information see www.magmatrek.it). The less energetic can retreat to the long, flat beaches of black sand to the north of the jetty, stone and shingly sand to the south. For refreshment, whether it's a mulberry *granita*, coffee or a full-blown meal, try **Il Canneto**, see 3, uphill from the port.

Salina

Peaceful **Salina** 5 is just a 25-minute boat hop from Lípari. Unlike the other islands, Salina is lush and fertile, producing Malvasia wine, a sweet golden dessert wine, and the capers which flavour many Aeolian dishes.

The highest point on the island is **Monte Fossa delle Felci**, one of Salina's two extinct thickly wooded volcanoes, which provides a lovely walk and fine views from the top (a 2–4 hour ascent depending on

Pretty Panarea

Food and drink

① La Nassa

Via G. Franza 36, Lípari; www.lanassa.it; €€

Expect a warm welcome and genuine Aeolian cuisine in this family-run restaurant. Local fish dominates the menu and full use is made of local produce: capers from Lípari, ricotta from Vulcano and Malvasia wine.

② Il Filippino

Piazza Municipio; www.filippino.it; €€€€

This superb fish restaurant flows out onto a flowery terrace overlooking the main town and harbour. Delicacies include fish risotto and *zuppa di pesce* (fish soup).

③ Il Canneto

Via Roma 47, Strómboli; tel: 392 709 7165; €€

Fish specialities here include *involtini di pesce spada* (swordfish rolled and stuffed), *spaghetti alla strombolana* (with anchovies and capers) and *tonno in agrodolce* (sweet and sour tuna). It's also open all day for coffee, delicious *granite* (flavoured crushed ice), ice cream and pastries.

④ Da Alfredo

Piazza Marina Grande, Lingua, Salina; tel: 090 984 3075; €

On the spacious seafront, this laidback café is famous for *granite*. Choose from pistachio, watermelon, mulberry and even mango (grown on the island by returnees from Australia), but the firm favourite is *granita alla mandorla* (with almonds). If hungry, tuck into *pane cunzato*, a giant toasted open sandwich with a mountain of local ingredients such as grilled aubergine, capers, mint and ricotta. More sophisticated fare is on offer at their little restaurant (Alfredo in Cucina) around the corner.

the route). The island has become increasingly chic over the last few years.

Ferries and hydrofoils dock at **Santa Marina di Salina**, an attractive back little port and village with an increasing number of chichi boutiques. (Some boats also stop at the even prettier and thoroughly laid-back fishing port of **Rinella**.)

The closest village is **Lingua**, 3km (2 miles) away, accessible by bus or by foot along the rocky palm-lined coast. There is not a lot here apart from a salt lagoon and small beach, but it has a sunny spacious waterfront and sea-view cafés, including the popular **Da Alfredo**, see ④. The main town is **Malfa**, 7km (4.5 miles) from Santa Marina Salina, where you can taste Malvasia, a golden dessert wine made from sun-dried grapes and still produced by small growers on the island.

Feisty Strómboli

Salina coastline

DIRECTORY

Our edit of the best hotels, restaurants and evening entertainment to suit all tastes and budgets, plus an A–Z of all the essential information you need to know, a quick language guide, and some great book and film recommendations to give you a flavour of the island.

Accommodation

Sicily has plentiful accommodation, with a choice ranges from the grand hotels of Palermo, Catania and Taormina to hip country retreats, stylish boutique hotels and simple B&Bs, rooms on farms, and town, island and beach apartments. Accommodation in the interior is thinner on the ground, except in the Aeolian Islands and the chic Val di Noto. Book ahead for popular destinations such as Taormina, Cefalù and Siracusa, especially during Easter and summer. The same applies to hotels on the offshore islands. Many resorts close in winter; some hotels and *agriturismi* insist on half or full board during high season.

Agriturismi or farm stays are generally delightful and good value. Some of these might be rural estates, country houses or rural apartments rather than farms. Etna has several rifugi, perfect for early morning starts and hearty evening meals. Villa rental is now big business thanks to foreign villa owners and design-conscious locals.

Price categories

Price for a double room including breakfast during high season:
€€€€ = over €300
€€€ = €200–300
€€ = €100–200
€ = under €100
Hotels in some of the larger cities now charge a tourist tax of €2–5 per person over 12 years of age for the first five consecutive nights. This applies to private self-catering accommodation as well as hotels.

Palermo

BB22

Palazzo Pantelleria, Largo Cavalieri di Malta 22; www.bb22.it; €€

This unique B&B has an excellent location in the historic centre, tucked behind San Domenico and close to the Vucciria Market. The seven guest rooms are individually furnished with plenty of designer chic. There are several more rooms in a beautifully restored palazzo a few minutes' walk away.

Palazzo Planeta

Via Principe di Belmonte 68, Palermo; www.planetaestate.it; €€

Spacious, beautifully designed apartments in a palazzo belonging to the Planeta family of winemakers (many of whom still live here too). The location is excellent – just off the main Via Roma – and fully equipped kitchens make them a very good choice for families or foodies keen to cook with the excellent produce of Palermo's markets.

Grand Hotel des Palmes

Grand Hotel des Palmes

Via Roma 398; www.grandhoteldespalmes.com; €€€€

This landmark hotel, splendidly restored in recent years, is in a great location for exploring the historic centre and elegant new Palermo. Famous former guests range from Lucky Luciano to Richard Wagner, who completed *Parsifal* here in 1882. Belle Epoque flourishes remain, as does the Art Nouveau lobby – Wagner completed *Parsifal* here in 1882.

Grand Hotel Piazza Borsa

Via dei Cartari 18; www.piazzaborsa.it; €€€€

Opened in 2010, this atmospheric hotel in the heart of the city combines a former monastery, church and cloisters as well as several ancient palazzi, including the former stock exchange. Among the highlights are a spa, spacious bedrooms, a bar in the cloisters, a winter garden and a gourmet restaurant in an Art Nouveau setting.

Palazzo Conte Federico

Via dei Biscottari 4; www.contefederico.com; €€

Run by a Palermitan count and his opera-singing Austrian wife, this palace in the heart of town offers an intriguing insight into Sicilian life. The apartments, all with private bathrooms, lead off the 17th-century courtyard.

Villa Igiea

Salita Belmonte 43; www.villa-igiea.com; €€€€

This glorious grand art nouveau villa on the seaside at Acquasanta just 3km (2 miles) north of the city centre, provides a perfect retreat in surroundings that were once home to the island's Florio family (of tuna and wine fame).Recently restored, it is run with panache by the Roccoo Forte group, and is buzzing with life and goodwill Facilities include leisurely trips on the villa boat, a beach club, swimming pool, tennis courts and a shuttle bus service to Palermo.

Mondello

Mondello Palace

Viale Principe di Scalea; www.mondellopalacehotel.it; €€€€

Palermo's favourite seaside retreat is the setting for this luxurious hotel. On the seafront and surrounded by a garden, it offers good-sized rooms, most with sea views. Facilities include a private beach, swimming pool, restaurant and bar. Reserve well ahead in summer.

Splendid La Torre

Via Piano Gallo 11; www.latorre.com; €€

A modern hotel on the rocky point of the bay at the quieter end of Mondello Lido. Own beach, pool and tennis courts, and sea or garden views from the rooms. There is also a restaurant serving delicious fish dishes.

Cefalù

Baia del Capitano

Contrada Mazzaforno; www.baiadelcapitano.it; €€€

This low key resort has a lovely setting amid gardens and olive groves above the

The Palazzo Conte Federico

sea about 5km (3 miles) west of Cefalù. The more expensive rooms have terrace gardens and sea views. A nearby beach is accessible on foot or by free hotel shuttle, and the hotel has its own swimming pool.

Kalura

Via Vincenzo Cavallaro 13, Caldura; www.hotelkalura.com; €€€

Ensconced in Mediterranean foliage, 3km (2 miles) from Cefalù, the Kalura offers clean and spacious rooms, most with a terrace and sea view. This is a family-friendly place with a spacious pool and children's pool, private beach, mountain bikes to hire and water sports nearby.

Scopello

La Tavernetta

Via Armando Diaz 3; tel: 0924 541 129; www.albergolatavernetta.it; €€

Friendly little hotel in a pretty coastal village near the Zíngaro nature reserve. Most of the rooms have balconies and sea views. Half board, which is good value, is compulsory in high season, but book well in advance.

Trápani

Ai Lumi

Corso Vittorio Emanuele 71; www.ailumi.it; €€

In the historic heart of town, this is an atmospheric, family-run B&B within an 18th-century palazzo. Rooms with kitchenette, private bathroom and Wi-Fi surround a splendid courtyard. It has the distinct advantage of being in the same building (and under the same management) as the best restaurant in town (see page 54), with a 15 percent discount for B&B guests.

B&B Porta delle Botteghelle

Via Serisso 31; www.portadellebotteghelle.it; €

Part of a building dating from the second half of the 19th century, this small bed-and-breakfast has been fully renovated and equipped with modern comforts and technology. The rooms are simple but full of character, with wooden ceilings and design furniture, and the hotel is conveniently located a few steps away from the harbour.

Cortile Antico

Vicolo Compagni 10 (traversa via Poeta Calvino); www.cortileantico.com; €

An old building arranged around an ancient courtyard is the setting of this small hotel, offering one-room and two-room apartments in the heart of the city. The patio has a local flavour, recalling old Sicily, while the interior is modern and comfortable, with design furniture and a variety of services and accessories.

La Gancia Residence

Piazza Mercato del Pesce; www.lagancia.com; €€

Just on the sea, this welcoming residence offers splendid views of the Mediterranean. Formerly a Carmelite convent, it was restored and turned into a modern hotel, offering modern studio apartments (no cooking facilities). Some of the apartments have marvellous terraces.

Villa Igiea

Erice

Elimo

Via Vittorio Emanuele 75; www.hotelelimo.it; €€€

This cosy 17th-century palazzo in the old town is a perfect retreat from the mists of mountain-top Erice, the ideal place from which to savour the citadel's other worldly atmosphere. Public areas are dotted with antiques and modern art, and there are lovely views from the roof terrace and many of the guest rooms.

Moderno

Via Vittorio Emanuele 67; www.hotelmodernoerice.it; €€

The excellent restaurant, renowned for its fish couscous, draws tourists and locals to the Moderno. Those who stay on enjoy a well-run, intimate hotel. Furnishings include antiques, country pieces and the hand-woven rugs for which Erice is famous.

Mazara del Vallo

Mahara Hotel

Lungomare San Vito 3; www.maharahotel.it; €€

This great-value four-star hotel on the seafront occupies an old Marsala wine warehouse. Rooms have views of the gardens and pool or the seafront. Facilities include a wellness centre, fish restaurant and free shuttle bus to the beach.

Agrigento

Colleverde Park

Passeggiata Archeologica; https://colleverdehotel.it; €€

Balcony view at Villa Athena

This quiet and welcoming hotel is situated at the start of Strada Panoramica. The 48 rooms are modern and the lush park surrounding the hotel offers lovely views of the Valley of Temples. It also houses a reasonable restaurant serving seasonal dishes.

Foresteria Baglio della Luna

Via Serafino Amabile Guastella 1; www.bagliodellaluna.com; €€€€

Set in the countryside, this traditional family-run Sicilian manor house *(baglio)* has been exquisitely restored and furnished with Sicilian antiques and paintings. Bedrooms are divided between the guesthouse and the ancient watchtower. The hotel features charming courtyards, a lush garden and solarium with Jacuzzi. It also has a noted restaurant.

Belmond Villa Sant'Andrea

Breakfast with a view

Tre Torri

Viale Cannatello 7; www.hoteltretorri.eu; €€

This large 3-star hotel is conveniently situated just east of the temples and at walking distance from the centre of Agrigento. There is a restaurant, a bar, indoor and outdoor swimming pools, and a very pleasant sauna.

Villa Athena

Via Passeggiata Archeologica 33; www.hotelvillaathena.it; €€€€

This five star hotel has a wonderful setting amid gardens and olive trees in the Valley of the Temples. Most of the comfortably furnished rooms have balconies overlooking the pool and Temple of Concordia. This is one of Sicily's most popular hotels, so be sure to book well in advance.

Piazza Armerina

Park Hotel Paradiso

Contrada Ramalda; www.parkhotelparadiso.it; €€

This hotel boasts friendly owners and a convenient location for visiting the famous mosaics at Villa Romana. Surrounded by a pine and eucalyptus forest it has spacious guest rooms, large swimming pool and pleasant surrounding park.

Villa Trigona

Contrada Bauccio; www.villatrigona.it; €€

The noble Trigona family's baronial country villa outside Piazza Armerina is now an engaging B&B packed with old-world charm. Don't miss the wonderful, good-value dinner, which uses locally-sourced produce. There is also a swimming pool with solarium.

Siracusa

Dimora delle Balze

SS287, nr Palazzolo Acreide; www.dimoradellebalze.com; €€€

A wonderful country house hotel, which makes a perfect base for seeing Siracusa, Noto and the rest of the Val di Noto. With just 11 rooms in an 18th century *masseria* (estate farmhouse) its extensive gardens, a big pool, spa and restaurant make a very nice place to escape to indeed.

Domus Mariae

Via Vittorio Veneto 76; www.domusmariaebenessere.com; €€€

Set in a restored ancient building in the historic centre, this small hotel with 12 rooms is run by nuns, who offer a warm welcome and good service.

Giuggiulena

Via Pitagora da Reggio 35; www.giuggiulena.it; €€

Stylish family-friendly B&B fused to the golden cliffs in the Borgata quarter of mainland Siracusa, a 20-minute walk (or quick bus ride) from both Ortigia and the ancient sites. Wonderful home-made breakfasts, sea-views from every room, and a door opening straight onto the flat rocks below – for some fantastic snorkelling (masks and sea-shoes provided).

Gutowski

Lungomare di Levante 26; tel: 0931 465 861; www.guthotel.it; €€

The Giardino di Costanza near Salemi

This comfortable hotel on the sea in Ortigia has 26 rooms in two late 19th-century buildings, and a small sunny terrace with panoramic views where they serve a delicious chocolate *granita*. Facilities include a restaurant (evenings only), free bikes and beach parasols.

Henry's House Hotel

Via del Castello Maniace 68, Siracusa; www.hotelhenryshouse.com; €€

Flamboyant Baroque decor in an Ortigia town house close to Castello Maniace, and with a terrace overlooking the (usually) calm waters of the Porto Grande (famed for its sunsets). Rooms are very comfy, public areas full of fascinating antiques, and breakfasts are generous.

Palazzo Artemide

Via Roma 66, Ortigia, Siracusa; www.vretreats.com; €€

There has been a hotel in this pale pink palazzo backing onto Ortigia's Duomo, since 1880. It re-opened in 2024 after a major renovation, and rooms are extremely comfy, with the same gold, midnight blue and grey décor throughout. There is a restaurant and bar – and in good weather dining is outside.

Palazzo del Sale

Via Santa Teresa 25, Ortigia; tel: 0931 65958; www.palazzodelsale.com; €€

Set in a former salt workshop, this quirky but upmarket B&B is convenient for exploring the most atmospheric part of Siracusa: the island of Ortigia.

Noto

La Casa di Montalbano

Corso Aldo Moro 44; tel: 393 9261 307; www.lacasadimontalbano.com; €

At least half the guests here are Montalbano fans since this B&B doubles as the Inspector's (TV) home. Simply furnished, it has just four rooms, good breakfasts and a great setting right on the beach of the pretty seaside village of Punta Secca (or Marinella as it's called in the TV series). Book well in advance.

Masseria degli Ulivi

Strada Statale 287; www.masseriadegliulivi.com; €€

Part of an old farm estate, this *masseria* (farmhouse) and spa located in the Noto countryside is the perfect spot for those looking to spend some quiet time in a beautiful bucolic setting. Guest rooms are furnished with taste, and there is a good swimming pool. The restaurant serves local dishes and uses produce from the kitchen garden.

Q92

Ronco Bernardo Leanti; www.q92notohotel.com; €€€€

Sumptuous yet hip hotel – with more than a splash of decadence – in the heart of Noto with wonderful views from balconies of one of the most striking townscapes in Sicily. Super-stylish rooms gorgeously designed and furnished public rooms, and a service style that is more host than hotel. Wonderful breakfasts.

A suite at the Giardino di Costanza

A more traditional room

Suite at Q92

San Carlo Suites
Corso Vittorio Emanuele 127; www.sancarlosuites.com; €€€

Upscale B&B on the main Corso of Noto, with wonderful views from balconies. Rooms are elegant and stylish, using antique pieces in a contemporary key and beds (with linen sheets) are very comfy indeed. Great care is taken over the breakfast, which features home-made cakes and excellent local hams and cheeses.

Seven Rooms Villadorata
Via Nicolaci 18; www.7roomsvilladorata.it; €€€€

Set in grandiose Palazzo Nicolaci, this divine boutique B&B respects the 18th-century spirit of the palace. The seven rooms, all with balconies, overlook the cathedral, and are decorated with fine furnishings. Views from the terrace, where are sublime. Wonderful breakfasts served at a communal table offer a good opportunity to meet other guests.

Villadorata Country House
Contrada Portelle, nr Noto; €€€€

Contemporary country house hotel with just 15 gracious and elegant rooms in lodges scattered around a vast hilly grove of olive, almond and citrus trees (access by electric golf cart). Some have their own private pool. Breakfasts are served at the table, and include what may be the best pastries you will eat anywhere outside Paris. There is also an excellent restaurant.

Villa Mediterranea
Viale Lido, Lido di Noto; www.villamediterranea.it; €€

While accommodation in old Noto is hard to come by, you'll find several places to stay in Lido di Noto, on the sea about 6km (4 miles) east of the town. The Villa Mediterranea, across the road from the beach, is one of the most pleasant, with simple but comfortable modern rooms and airy sea views.

Modica

Casa Talia
Via Exaudinos 1, Modica; www.casatalia.it; €€€€

Chic accommodation in an artfully-converted cluster of traditional old stone houses with fantastic views of Modica. Created by two Milanese architects, décor fuses Sicilian Baroque with touches of North Africa. Breakfast is served on the terrace, while the star of the public

Reading room at Caol Ishka in Siracusa

rooms is a cavernous whitewashed former water cistern (a perfect place to read a book on a sultry day). There are plans to open a pool in 2026.

Ferro Hotel

Via Stazione SN. www.ferrohotelmodica.it; €€

This is a modern station hotel converted from a dormitory for railway workers and trains are the dominant theme. Guest rooms are comfortable and contemporary, with sound-proofing.

Il Cavaliere

Corso Umberto I, 259; https://palazzoilcavaliere.com; €

On the main street of Módica, this is a lovely B&B with friendly owners set in an elegant early 19th-century palazzo. Rooms are individually furnished and retain original features such as frescoes and exposed stonework.

Pietre Nere Resort

Pietre Nere, Via Pietre Nere Cava Ispica 142; www.pietrenereresort.it; €€€

This resort and spa features 28 rooms overlooking the Módica countryside, and is located less than 1 km away from the archaeological area of Ispica. Rooms are modern and classy, with a prevalence of white and black. Facilities include a restaurant and swimming pool.

Ragusa

Artemisia Resort

Via E. Caruso 13; https://en.artemisiaresort.com; €€

In the countryside on the outskirts of Ragusa, this lovely boutique hotel is cared for by gracious owners who also run a noted *pasticceria*, hence delicious Módica-style pastries for breakfast. Hang by the pool, explore the Montalbano Detective Trail (ask for a map) or head to the nearby beach.

Locanda Don Serafino

Via XI Febbraio 15, Ragusa Ibla; www.locandadonserafino.it; €€€€

This inviting boutique hotel, excavated from the rock face, houses 10 elegant guest rooms and suites. The renowned restaurant with two Michelin stars, is 10 minutes' walk away (see page 117).

Risveglio Ibleo

Largo Camerina 3, Ragusa Ibla; tel: 0932 247 811; www.risveglioibleo.com; €

This 19th-century palazzo has been converted into a B&B with three self-catering rooms. The owner takes pride in serving breakfast in his own dining room: Arab biscuits, thyme-flavoured *dolce*, fresh ricotta and bread with home-made marmalade and Ragusa honey.

Chiaramonte Gulfi

Antica Stazione

Via Madonna Santissimo Rosario, SP n. 8, Km 3; www.anticastazione.com; €

Set in the Iblei mountains, this hugely friendly, family-run hotel was once a railway station. Although convenient for both Ragusa and Chiaramonte, the hotel feels peacefully aloof, set among

Hotel Signum

carob trees. Warm, professional service is complemented by quiet rooms, a very popular restaurant and low prices.

Valle di Chiaramonte

Contrada Piano Zacchi – Pantanelli; www.valledichiaramonte.it; €

This friendly *agriturismo* is made up of clusters of rustic self-catering apartments. Guests can enjoy the farm-grown produce, from aromatic olive oil to salami, cooked meats and mature Ragusano DOP cheese.

Catania

5 Balconi B&B

Via Plebiscito 133; www.5balconi.it; €

On the second floor of a palazzo (with lift) and close to the castle, this welcoming B&B has three cosy guest rooms, one with a volcano view. The rooms share a bathroom and shower room. Rob (English) and Cristina (Sicilian) are hugely helpful hosts and will tell you all about the region over the delicious breakfast.

Donna Carmela

Contrada Grotte 5, Carruba di Riposto; tel: 095 809 383; www.donnacarmela.com; €€€

This charming hotel is set in a historic villa built in the 1800s, but has very modern interiors, and stylish contemporary suites scattered around its subtropical gardens. The owners cultivate flowers for sale, and offer guided tours to their Mediterranean flora greenhouses and fields. Good restaurant with a menu based on local specialities from the Catania area.

EH13 B&B

Via Sant'Euplio 13; tel: 095 715 2216; www.eh13.it; €€

This boutique bed-and-breakfast is furnished with a mix of designer furniture, ethnic objects, Baroque-inspired pieces and high-quality technological accessories. Conveniently located in the heart of Catania's historic centre, this hotel also offers magnificent views of Mount Etna. Breakfast is traditional Sicilian featuring organic local ingredients.

Etnea 316

Via Etnea 316; www.hoteletnea316catania.com; €

A refurbished B&B that offers a lovely home-away-from-home feeling, with spacious, traditional rooms and a welcoming atmosphere.

UNA Hotel Palace

Via Etnea 218; tel: 095 250 5111; www.unahotels.it; €€€

Part of the UNA chain, this is a luxury hotel on the main shopping street. The 94 rooms' decor is minimalist with bold colours. Locals flock to the roof garden bar for *aperitivi* with views of Etna.

Taormina

Ashbee

Viale S. Pancrazio; www.theashbeehotel.com; €€€€

Looking out to the Ionian sea and across to Mount Etna this hotel was originally the Villa San Giorgio, built in 1907

San Domenico Palace

by Arts and Crafts Architect Charles Robert Ashbee for an Englishman living in Sicily. Small, elegant and exclusive, it boasts a spectacular infinity pool, a garden of palms, lush lawn and statues and an English-style restaurant with a Michelin star. The rooftop lounge is a lovely spot at sunset.

Belmond Grand Hotel Timeo

Via Teatro Greco 59; www.belmond.com; €€€€

Set beside the Teatro Greco, Sicily's grandest hotel is impeccably run by the Belmond group and has been restored to its original splendour. Airy, sophisticated suites have wonderful views over terraced gardens and the sea. A shuttle runs to the private beach at its sister hotel in summer. It also boasts a gastronomic restaurant (see page 86).

Belmond Villa Sant'Andrea

Via Nazionale 137, Taormina €€€€

Seaside hotels don't come much better than this. What began life as a Sicilian villa belonging to a Cornish engineer is now an elegant establishment of 71 rooms, all of which have sea views. Service is unfailingly charming, and the food superb. In good weather breakfast, lunch and dinner (all superb) are eaten on a terrace overlooking the beach.

San Domenico Palace

Piazza San Domenico 5; tel: 0942 613 111; www.san-domenico-palace.com; €€€€

The HBO series, *White Lotus*, was filmed in this former Dominican monastery following a multi-million-euro restoration by the Four Seasons group. It's a splendid, romantic and unique place, with super-luxe contemporary rooms contrasting with the romance of several cloisters and gorgeous gardens Views are magnificent, especially from the terrace towards Etna and the sea. Cuisine is outstanding, service faultless.

Taodomus

Corso Umberto 224, Taormina; www.hoteltaodomustaormina.com; €€€

Scrupulously clean rooms in an early 20th century townhouse on Taormina's main Corso. Highlight is the roof terrace with views up to Etna and over the vast bay below, where breakfast and evening cocktails are served.

Hotel Villa Ducale

Via Leonardo da Vinci 60, Taormina; www.villaducale.com; €€€

There are spectacular views from this intimate boutique hotel on the upper edge of Taormina, far from the madding crowds of the city centre. Heart of the hotel is the panoramic covered terrace (the perfect place to sip a cocktail at sunset). Food is excellent and breakfast exceptionally generous.

Villa Belvedere

Via Bagnoli Croce 79; www.villabelvedere.it; €€€

This inviting villa hotel with stunning views sits on a hillside just above the botanical gardens, with semi-

Ornate Noto balcony

Belmond Grand Hotel Timeo

tropical grounds surrounding a lavish swimming pool. Most rooms have a balcony or terrace – those in the villa, the older section of the hotel, are especially atmospheric with intricate terracotta flooring and antique furnishings aplenty.

Villa Fiorita

Via Pirandello 39; www.villafioritahotel.com; €€€

This lovely hotel is located on the hillside edging the town. There are 25 pleasant rooms, many with wonderful views overlooking the Mediterranean. Lush garden and a terrace with lounge chairs. No children.

Villa Greta

Via Leonardo da Vinci 46; www.villagreta.it; €€€

A small, family-run hotel where most most rooms come with a balcony and incredible views. It's a 15-minute walk from Taormina on the Castelmola road and about 800 m from the cable car.

Villa Schuler

Piazzetta Bastione 16; www.hotelvillaschuler.com; €€€

This villa hotel, which has been in the same family since 1905, serves up elegant old-world charm and splendid views of Etna and the Bay of Naxos. Rooms overlook the large subtropical garden or out to sea (rates vary accordingly). A minimum two-night stay is required during high season. Free bikes are available for guests.

Villa Taormina

Via Fazzello 49; www.hotelvillataormina.com; €€€€

A charming boutique hotel, with rooms full of antiques in the traditional style of a Sicilian luxury home. The hotel also has a lovely terrace and garden with magnificent view of the sea and the hills, parking and a shuttle service to the beach.

Aeolian Islands

Capofaro Malvasia & Resort

Via Faro 3, Salina; www.capofaro.it; €€€€

This feels like the essence of the Mediterranean in its sublime sea and mountain views, with rooms and suites in traditional-style whitewashed Aeolian houses scattered among the vineyards from which Tasca d'Almerita's Malvasia is made.

Diana Brown

Vico Himera 3, Lípari; tel: 090 981 2584; www.dianabrown.it; €€

Run by a friendly South African-Sicilian couple, this B&B five minutes' walk from the port has 12 refurbished rooms (five with self-catering facilities) and a lovely roof terrace.

Gattopardo Park

Viale Diana, Lipari; tel: 0909 811 035; www.gattopardoparkhotel.it; €€

Located near the centre of Lípari, this 18th-century villa offers a marvellous swimming pool and private bungalows. Open Mar–Oct.

The pool at Hotel Signum

Giardino sul Mare

Via Maddalena 65, Lipari; www.giardinosulmare.it; €€€

This small hotel is on the sea and not far from the centre of Lípari. The views are great, breakfast is reasonable, and there is also a pleasant swimming pool and a direct access to sea.

Hotel Ravesi

Via Roma 66, Malfa, Salina; https://hotelravesi.it; €€€€

A true dream of hotel which seamlessly combines the personal service of a family-run establishment with easy Aeolian luxury. Gorgeous rooms in pretty yellow Aeolian houses set lush gardens with unforgettable views over the sea to the islands of Panarea and Stromboli. Add to that breakfasts home-made by Mrs Ravesi; boat trips in the hotel's own boat with a sunset aperitivo on board; and gourmet cocktails with an array of homemade delicacies, and you may wish you never had to leave.

Hotel Rocce Azzurre

Via Maddalena 69, Lípari; www.hotelrocceazzurre.it; €€

This hotel on the water's edge has restful, refurbished rooms and gorgeous sea views. The bathing platform with sunbeds is perfect for chilling out. Half board only in peak season.

Lisca Bianca

Via San Petro, Panarea; www.liscabianca.it; €€€

Situated right in front of the tourist harbour, this hotel has 25 rooms (each with a balcony), a beach and a swimming pool. The grounds are large and lush. Open Apr–end-Oct.

Balcony at Villa Ducale

Raya

Via San Pietro, Panarea; www.hotelraya.it; €€€€

This landmark hotel is at once contemporary and timeless, set on the most chic island in the Aeolians yet still laidback and effortlessly charming. A favourite among celebrities.

Signum

Via Scalo 15, Malfa, Salina; www.hotelsignum.it; €€€€

This luxury hotel hidden away in the heart of the little village of Malfa, boasts sea views, fragrant lemon and jasmine trees, and whitewashed interiors. With an infinity pool and spa natural hot springs, shady verandas and fine dining by the sea, you'll find it hard to tear yourself away.

Hammock with a view of Strómboli, Panarea

Restaurants

Sicily's ancient, distinguished cuisine is among the most pleasurable discoveries you'll make on the island. Sicilian chefs used to be snapped up by starry establishments abroad, but many of today's culinary talents are now showcasing their skills at home. Along with the grand gastronomic restaurants, there are wonderful street snacks – especially in the markets, where some stalls will grill fish, squid and octopus while you wait. And between the two, you'll find plenty of *trattorie* serving authentic Sicilian dishes.

The southeast of the island, especially Ragusa, is the current culinary hotspot, with some of the most varied and creative cooking in Sicily. Palermo and Catania both have excellent and diverse restaurants, and sophisticated Taormina has an array of gastronomic tables. Prices here are higher than anywhere else on the island.

Lunch is usually served from 1pm to 3pm and dinner from 8pm to 10.30pm or later. Nearly all restaurants display a menu outside with prices. Beware of the fixed-price menus in tourist resorts, which are often poor value, and instead try to pick restaurants which are frequented by locals. Most restaurant bills include a service charge (usually 10 percent) and many add a *coperto* (cover charge) as well. See also Food and Drink, page 16, and the food and drink boxes throughout the Best Routes section.

Price categories

Price for a two-course meal for one person, including a glass of wine and service:

€€€€ = over €80
€€€ = €50–80
€€ = €25–50
€ = under €25

Palermo

Al Covo dei Beati Paoli

Piazza Marina 50; www.alcovodeibeatipaoli.it; €€

With tables set out on Palermo's prettiest piazza, this is a pleasant spot in summer. In winter, guests can enjoy the medieval-inspired interior. Appetisers include *caponata* and lamb skewers, and the baked suckling kid is delicious. The pizzas are good, but service can be slow.

Antico Caffè Spinnato

Via Principe di Belmonte 115; www.spinnato.it; €

Located in a chic, central pedestrianised zone, this is where the smart set come for *aperitivi*. The Spinnato group is known for its superb ice creams, *cassata*, sumptuous cakes and *Cannoli*, served here and at Piazza Castelnuovo 5). Pastas, grills and salads are also available.

Sicilian caponata

Gigi Mangia

Via Principe di Belmonte 104; www.gigimangiaristorante.it; €€

Set on an elegant pedestrianised street, this is a *trattoria* with a delicatessen attached that delivers food and wine worldwide. Menu highlights include a selection of delicious vegetarian appetisers and *colonnello piero va a favignana* – a pasta dish with tomatoes, herbs and *bottarga* (tuna roe).

Osteria dei Vespri

Piazza Croce dei Vespri 6; www.osteriadeivespri.it; €€€€

This old tavern occupies the former coach house of 18th-century Palazzo Gangi. It's set on a lovely, sheltered square with tables outdoors in summer. The cooking is creative Italian, with artfully presented dishes. Try ravioli stuffed with baked ricotta, fried courgettes and lemon served with *bottarga* (dried and salted tuna roe), followed by fresh fish or meat (suckling pig, quail or beef). The wine list has more than 350 labels to choose from.

Mondello

Alle Terrazze

Via Regina Elena; www.alleterrazze.it; €€€€

Set in an Art Nouveau beach establishment, this gracious spot is particularly good for fish. The chef pays particular attention to ingredient selection, and even the bread is baked in-house. Well-stocked wine cellar and impeccable service. Book ahead.

Bye Bye Blues

Via del Garofalo 23; www.byebyeblues.it; €€€€

Don't be put off by the nightclub name – this gastronomic restaurant on the road into Mondello is superb. A minimalist dining room (simple black chairs, plain white walls) is the setting for Patrizia di Benedetto's Michelin-starred Mediterranean cuisine, presented with plenty of flair. Typical dishes include prawn carpaccio and squid salad, Sicilian cheese soufflé or black lasagne with codfish and pumpkin purée.

Cefalù

Kentia al Trappitu

Via Calo Ortolani di Bordonaro 96; tel: 0921 423 801; €€

Known for its charm, cuisine and lovely terrace overlooking the sea. The fish arrives daily and the meat menu is rich and interesting. Sample the *scaloppine ai funghi* (mushroom and veal escalope) and *panzerotti di magro* (fried ravioli filled with ricotta and spinach).

L'Antica Corte

Cortile Pepe 7; tel: 0921 423 228; €€

Fresh fish and pastas topped with seafood-based sauces are favourites on the menu in this old-town restaurant. The best seating is in the charming courtyard.

Lo Scoglio Ubriaco

Via Carlo Ortolani di Bordonaro 2; tel: 0921 423 370; €–€€

The handsome terrace here overlooks the harbour, so you can watch the

Fresh seafood is a popular choice

fishing boats while enjoying *spaghetti al cartoccio di mare* (spaghetti with seafood, sealed in a bag and baked), plus grilled or fried fish. Pizzas are served in the evenings.

Monreale

Bricco & Bacco

Via B. D'Acquisito 13, Monreale; https://briccoebacco.com; €€€

This is a haven for carnivores with a great mixed grill. There is no fish or pasta – but excellent antipasti and mouth-watering desserts. Other plus points are a warm, friendly atmosphere, attentive service and good wines to complement the meat.

Castelbuono

Nangalarruni

Via della Confraternite 7; www.hostarianangalarruni.it; €€€

Well-known chef Giuseppe Carollo showcases the best ingredients from the Madonie mountains, using everything from mushrooms to suckling pig and sheep's cheese. Wash it down with wine from the Santa Anastasia estate in the hills below town.

Alcamo

Sirignano Wine Resort

Contrada Sirignano; www.sirignanowineresort.it; €€

Set among rolling vineyards 12km (7.5 miles) from Alcamo, this appealing wine resort is home to a remarkable chef who creates wonderful interpretations of classic Sicilian dishes with a delicate touch. Combine lunch with a wine tasting and tour around the organic winery, or even fall into one of the cosy beds. Lunch and visits with reservation only (meals are mainly lunch, but dinner is possible on request).

Trápani

Caupona Taverna di Sicilia

Piazza Purgatorio 32; www.osteriacaupona.it; €€

The seafood here is superb: try the *caponata di pesce* (fish with aubergine, celery and capers in a sweet-and-sour sauce), *polpette al nero di sepia* (cuttlefish balls) or fish couscous. There's an excellent wine list too.

Taverna Paradiso

Lungomare D. Alighieri 22; tel: 0923 22303; €€€.

A highly regarded inn right on the seafront, specialising in *neonata*, *spaghetti ai ricci* (spaghetti with sea urchins), octopus salad and tuna. Lovely outdoor patio on the beach. It is advisable to book ahead.

Erice

La Pentolaccia

Via G.F. Guarnotti 17; www.ristorantelapentolaccia.it; €€

This restaurant in the centre of Erice occupies an old monastery. Dishes are all local, including some wonderful fish and couscous specials. Good choice of local wines.

Swordfish hors d'œuvre

Moderno

Via Vittorio Emanuele 67; www.hotelmodernoerice.it; closed Mon in quiet season; €€€

This charming family-run hotel restaurant serves classic Sicilian dishes including a delicious *caponata*. The décor is both elegant and sober and there is a beautiful terrace with panoramic views of the surrounding hills.

Monte San Giuliano

Vicolo San Rocco, 7, Erice; www.montesangiuliano.it; €€

This rustic-style inn has a delightful terraced garden and good traditional Trapanese cooking. Try *involtini di melanzana* (stuffed aubergine rolls), pasta with Trapanese pesto, fresh shrimp and artichokes, or grilled meats.

Marinella di Selinunte

Africa da Bruno

Via Alceste 24, Marinella di Selinunte; tel: 388 371 2814; €

This is a simple summertime eatery with no sea views but excellent-value antipasti, pasta, fish and, in the evenings, pizzas al legno (in a wood-burning oven).

Pierrot

Via Marco Polo 108, Marinella di Selinunte; tel: 092 446 205; €€

Come in season for fabulous sea views, fish of the day and pizzas. Specialities are *trenette ai ricci* (pasta with sea urchins), *spaghetti ai gamberi con asparagi e rucola* (with prawns, asparagus and rocket) and chargrilled fish.

Agrigento

La Promenade dei Templi

Via Passeggiata Archeologica 12–14; tel: 0922 24283; €€

Situated between the temples and the town, the café and *pasticceria* are known for their almond treats: tuck into cakes, marzipan treats, *granite*, ice cream and *latte di mandorla* (a milky almond drink), while the restaurant serves fish and meat dishes. Lovely terraces in the front and in the back.

Trattoria Concordia

Via Porcello 8; tel: 0922 22668; €€

Good for grilled fish and seafood-based pasta dishes – try the spaghetti with prawns, or those with swordfish, eggplant and mint. The house wine is good. There are also reasonably priced fixed menus and outdoor seating in the summer.

Licata

La Madia

Corso Filippo Re Capriata 22; www.ristorantelamadia.it; €€€€

Licata is a rather unprepossessing port town between Ragusa and Agrigento, but it boasts the island's most celebrated restaurant. Chef Pino Cuttaia delights with his inventive, two Michelin-starred cuisine. Typical is his version of *arancino* (a fried rice ball and classic Sicilian street snack) in a sauce of red mullet and wild fennel.

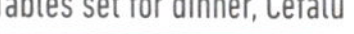

Tables set for dinner, Cefalù

Piazza Armerina

La Ruota

Contrada Paratore (near Villa Romana); www.trattorialaruota.it; €€

Housed in a converted watermill, this attractive *trattoria* specialises in home-made pasta. Try the delicious *maccheroni*, fresh tomato pasta and *melanzane in agrodolce* (aubergines in sweet-and-sour vinaigrette), followed by roast pork or rabbit. The fresh ricotta and *primosale* pecorino cheeses are delicious with a glass of Nero d'Avola or Cerasuola di Vittoria. Booking is advisable.

Da Totò

Via Mazzini 29, Piazza Armerina; tel: 0935 680 153; €€

This friendly, family-run trattoria located in the heart of Piazza Armerina is an excellent place to stop when passing through town en route to Villa Romana in nearby Casale. The menu reflects the mountain setting, with an emphasis on game, rabbit and other meat dishes. It's also a pizzeria in the evenings.

Siracusa

Don Camillo

Via Maestranza 96; www.ristorantedoncamillosiracusa.it; €€€

An old Ortigia favourite, this formal, rather old-fashioned restaurant serves some wonderful variations on local specialities, including pasta with cuttlefish in its own ink, *zuppa di mucco* (fish soup) or grilled tuna steak. The well-stocked cellar has a choice of 700 wines, with emphasis on Sicily. Reservations are recommended.

La Foglia

Via Capodieci 29, Ortigia; http://lafoglia.it; €€

Renowned more for its quirky decor and atmosphere (think dolls and chintz) than its cuisine, the restaurant is owned by a sculptor and is packed with paintings, statuary and mixed crockery. A limited menu offers soups, home-made pastas, vegetarian platters and seafood dishes.

Taverna Giudecca Ortigia

Via della Giudecca 7, Ortigia; www.tavernagiudecca.it; €

This small but welcoming trattoria specialises in what is known as *apericena*, a dinner made of tapa-like local specialties ranging from cured meats, cheese platters, baked ricotta and experimental recipes made with local ingredients. Great selection of Sicilian wines.

Noto

Pasticceria Kennedy

Via Silvio Spaventa 19; €

Noto's most popular bakery and pastry shop. Choose among *cannoli*, *cassate*, ricotta cheesecakes, candied fruits, chocolate, and much more. There is also a good selection of savoury snacks for the perfect lunch picnic.

Trattoria del Carmine

Via Ducezio 1; tel: 0931 838 705; €€

Everything at this simple, family-run trattoria is fresh and home-

Swordfish rolls (involtini di pesce spada)

made. Regional specialities include seafood-based pastas and *coniglio alla stimpirate*, a traditional Sicilian rabbit dish with a sweet-and-sour sauce. Pizzas are also served in the evening.

Ragusa

Baglio la Pergola

Piazza Luigi Sturzo, Contrada Selvaggiowww.baglio.it; €€€

Popular, elegant spot in the countryside outside Ragusa for updated versions of local dishes. Sample ricotta ravioli with a *ragú* of suckling pig, or the *maccheroncini* with the pistachio pesto. Second courses are mainly meaty, but some fish is listed on the menu too.

Locandina Don Serafino

Via Avvocato Ottaviano 13, Ragusa Ibla; www.locandadonserafino.it; L and D Tue–Sun; €€€€

Burrowed into the basement of an atmospheric mansion,and boasting a Michelin star, this is one of Sicily's most seductive restaurants. The delectable cuisine ranges from seafood salad to sophisticated interpretations of Sicilian street food (rice balls with saffron) or Ragusan rabbit. The boutique hotel is equally lovely (see page 107).

La Piazzetta

Piazza Duomo 14; www.lapiazzettaragusaibla.it; €€

Genuine *cucina ragusana* so grilled vegetables, *impanate* (Sicilian pasty), *cavatelli ragusani*, cheeses and an array of meats, but little fish. Wide selection of Sicilian and Italian wines including great Passitos.

Chiaramonte Gulfi

Antica Stazione

Contrada Santissimo; www.anticastazione.com; €

Set in an old railway station, this easygoing hotel trattoria and pizzeria (with a summer terrace) is popular with locals. Dishes use delicious Chiaramonte olive oil and Ragusan cheeses. The meat and fish set menus are both superb value.

Catania

Antica Sicilia

Via Rocaforte 15/17; www.ristoranteosteriaanticasicilia.it; €€

The display of fish and seafood lures customers into this popular and reasonably-priced trattoria. A large menu offers Sicilian fish specialities such as stuffed squid, pasta with sea urchins and *involtini di pesce spada* (swordfish rolls). It also has good pizzas baked in a wood oven.

La Cantinaccia

Via Calatafimi 1/a; tel: 095 537 291; €€€

This upmarket but intimate restaurant is designed in rustic style. The cuisine is international and Sicilian with pizza served in the evening. They also have a good selection of artisanal beers.

La Marchesana

Via Mazza 4; tel: 095 315 171; €€

The menu is particularly strong on fish at this small restaurant, and the

Anchovies in sea water

Sicilian sweets

friendly owners offer a warm welcome. Eat outside in fine weather, or inside in the elegant vaulted dining room.

Menza

Viale Mario Rapisardi 143; www.menza.it; €€

This is a typical Sicilian *rosticceria* with takeaway roast meats and street snacks: try the *arancini* (savoury filled rice balls), sweet *crespelle* (pancakes) with honey or the delicious pastries.

La Siciliana

Viale Marco Polo 52; www.lasiciliana.it; €€€

Set within a 19th-century villa, La Siciliana is quite a way north of the centre (and expensive by local standards), but it's well worth the trip. Specialities include roast lamb, carpaccio of fresh swordfish and imaginative vegetable dishes, served with good local wines. There is a smoking section. Reservations are required.

Trattoria Il Mare

Via S. Michele, 7; tel: 095 317024; €€

Just off the main tourist drag this family-run, simply-furnished trattoria has first-class seafood. The fish antipasti are a real feast.

Taormina

Al Duomo

Vico Ebrei 1; www. ristorantealduomotaormina.com; €€€

In the heart of the old town this is an atmospheric restaurant with a rustic-chic interior and a sought-after terrace overlooking Piazza Duomo. Try the hearty seafood cuisine, fresh fish or casseroled lamb and end with the *tortino di cioccolato*.

L'Arco dei Cappuccini

Via Cappuccini, 1, near Porta Messina; www.arcodeicappuccini.com; €€€

A busy, welcoming place with excellent Sicilian cooking with an emphasis on fresh fish. Good Sicilian wines and liqueurs. Reservations recommended.

Bella Blu

Via Luigi Pirandello 28; www. bellablutaormina.com; €€

This buzzing restaurant, pizzeria, piano bar and disco is an entertaining and chic place to spend an evening. Menu highlights include grills and barbecued meats, plus pasta with sardines. Reserve ahead in summer.

La Capinera

Via Nazionale 177; www.pietrodagostino. it/la-capinera/; Tue–Sun D; €€€€

Michelin-starred chef Pietro D'Agostino creates unique dishes with local, seasonal produce from all over Sicily. From the home-made breads to the fish dishes, this is an excellent choice.

La Giara

Vico la Floresta 1; tel: 0942 23360; €€€€

This respected restaurant and piano bar is also a popular nightlife destination among chic locals. The dining experience

Al fresco lunch in Taormina

is an elegant one, on roof or terraces with traditional menu and service. Advance booking strongly recommended.

Granduca

Corso Umberto I, 172; www.ristorantegranduca.it; €€€€

This restaurant and pizzeria offer lovely views over the bay and excellent Sicilian dishes, including home-made pastas topped with rich sauces of aubergine, capers and tuna, along with fresh fish dishes such as *involtini di spade alla griglia* – grilled swordfish rolls stuffed with breadcrumbs and parsley.

Mamma Rosa

Via Naumachie 10; www.mammarosataormina.com; €€

With tables lining the lively alley in the summer months, this busy spot serves up crispy pizzas, cooked in a wood-fired oven, as well as standard Italian fare.

Principe di Cerami

Hotel San Domenico Palace, Piazza San Domenico 5; www.principecerami.com; €€€€

This elegant gourmet restaurant, with two Michelin stars to its name, is set in the gorgeous San Domenico hotel, which was formerly a monastery. Dine on the terrace in summer.

Capri Leone (Messina)

Antica Filanda

Contrada Raviola; https://anticafilanda.me; €€

Overlooking the Aeolian Islands, this restaurant focuses on produce and dishes from the Nebrodi mountains. Expect the likes of black Nebrodi pork, Montalbano provola cheese, ricotta and Nebrodi goat's cheese.

Aeolian Islands

Capofaro

Via Faro 3, Salina; www.capofaro.it; €€€€

This romantic restaurant in a luxury hotel draws a chic, international moneyed crowd. The setting is elegant but relaxed, with a lovely terrace by the pool. If you're inspired by the cuisine (highly likely), consider booking one of the cookery classes.

Cincotta

Via San Pietro, Panarea; www.hotelcincotta.it; €€€€

Smart hotel with smart restaurant, where people dress down expensively and eat costly fish. The views are wonderful, and the cuisine is based on fish, with the freshest ingredients.

Hycesia

Via San Pietro, Panarea; www.hycesia.it; €€€

Named after the old word for Panarea, this chic spot near the port offers sophisticated, inventive cuisine, but still based on the catch of the day. Popular with the smart set. Great wine list.

Kasbah

Vico Selinunte 43, Lípari; tel: 090 921 5367; €€

This relaxed and fashionable eatery is popular for its outstanding pizzas, but also offers a tempting menu featuring authentic Sicilian fish dishes.

Waiting for customers

Sicilian Christmas pastries

Nightlife

Sicily may not be renowned for its nightclubs and discos, but Palermo, Catania and Siracusa offer a vibrant cultural scene, and there's no shortage of late-night bars in the main towns and coastal resorts. Taormina boasts the most sophisticated and expensive nightlife, ranging from summer dance clubs and live events at the Greek Theatre to aperitifs at elegant Etna-view bars or an evening *passeggiata* along the main street. Palermo pretty much empties out on summer evenings, when locals decamp to the fashionable beach resort of Mondello. Catania is the coolest and liveliest city for nightlife, with plenty of late-night bars and music venues. As an energetic university city it offers events such as from pop-rock spectaculars and open-air summer festivals.

Some of the most memorable performances – Greek plays, concerts, ballet, dance, jazz – are linked to the summer festivals, held from June to August. Check with local tourist boards for a list of events or look in the two main newspapers, *Il Giornale di Sicilia* and *La Sicilia*.

The following listings include cultural venues, plus a small selection of lively nightclubs and bars.

Palermo

Teatro Massimo

Piazza Verdi; www.teatromassimo.it

The opera house offers a wonderful programme of ballet and opera. Dominating Piazza Verdi, it is one of the grandest and largest opera houses in Europe. The last scenes of *The Godfather Part III* were filmed here. The opera season runs from late September to late June. Tickets to performances here are always in high demand. They can be bought online at www.ctbox.it (website is in Italian but easy to use).

Teatro Politeama Garibaldi

Piazza Ruggero Settimo; www.teatro.it/teatri/politeama-garibaldi-palermo-cartellone

This neoclassical-style theatre, home to Sicily's symphony orchestra the Orchestra Sinfonica Siciliana, stages classical concerts and ballet, plus occasional jazz and contemporary music

Lo Spasimo

Via dello Spasimo; tel: 091 740 8861

This atmospheric entertainment complex is set in a former 16th-century monastery and was one of the first projects during the regeneration of the La Kalsa quarter. Classical and jazz concerts are held in the cloisters and the roofless church – on a sultry, starry night, with the swaying palms in the background, the atmosphere is wonderfully romantic. Some of the events are free.

Teatro Massimo in Palermo

Antico Caffè Spinnato

Via Principe di Belmonte 107; www.spinnato.it

Via Principe di Belmonte is a chic, central pedestrianised zone where the smart set gather at alfresco bars for *aperitivi*. The elegant Antico Caffè Spinnato is the best-known venue, with a reputation for superb ice creams, *cassata* and *cannoli*. It's also a great people-watching spot.

Taormina

Morgana Bar

Scesa Morgana; www.morganataormina.it

This late-night cocktail bar, decorated in timewarp 1960s Surrealist style, has a tiny dancefloor and decent cocktails. Don't expect the action really to get going until midnight, then carry on partying until the doors close much, much later.

Teatro Greco

Via Teatro Greco 40; www.teatrogrecotaormina.com

Nothing beats a classical drama set in Taormina's stunning Greek Theatre, and visitors come from around the world for the annual summer arts festival in July and August. Performances include classical drama, opera, dance and music. Plays are staged in the original language.

Wunderbar

Piazza IX Aprile; https://wunderbarcaffe.com

Sip cocktails until the early hours of the morning and follow in the footsteps of Tennesse Williams, Greta Garbo and Elizabeth Taylor. The setting is glamorous and there are prices to match.

Catania

Mercati Generali

SS417; www.mercatigenerali.org

This converted warehouse set amid orange groves is a cult music venue. It's one of the few clubs in Sicily where you'll find top European DJs, live rock and pop. Summer partying in the courtyard hots up from around midnight nightly in summer. It's not an easy spot to get to, involving a 20-minute taxi ride from Catania.

Palazzo Scammacca

Piazza Scammacca; www.palazzoscammacca.it

Aristocratic palazzo belonging to to the Scammacca-Murgo family (famed for creating Sicily's finest *methode champagnoise* wines on Mount Etna) which hosts regular jazz concerts and jam sessions in its appropriately named bar, Monk.

Teatro Massimo Bellini

Via G. Perrotta 12; www.teatromassimobellini.it

Named after the famous operatic composer Bellini, the theatre opened in 1890 with his opera *Norma*. It's a major venue for opera, classical music and ballet. Tickets (available online) are highly sought after, especially for operas composed by Bellini himself.

Zò

Piazzale Asia 6; www.zoculture.it

This futuristic culture and arts centre, housed in an ex-sulphur refinery near Stazione Centrale, hosts concerts, films, club nights, cutting-edge theatre and offbeat art exhibitions.

Essentials

Accessible travel

Sicily is one of the worst places in Italy to get around for travellers with disabilities. Most churches and sites have steps, and few of the museums and archaeological sites have wheelchair access. Hotels of a certain size are required by law to have an accessible room, but in historic buildings access to the room itself may be impossible because of planning restrictions. Given the challenges, it is wise to book through a specialised tour operator who can offer customised tours and itineraries such as Disabled Holidays (www.disabledholidays.com).

Age restrictions

The minimum age for driving with a valid licence is 18, but many car-hire companies will not rent to anyone under 21. Drivers under 24 usually incur a surcharge.

Budgeting for your trip

Prices generally match those of mainland Italy, unless you are staying in the interior well off the beaten track. High season rates in luxury hotels by the sea and in the Aeolian islands can be stratospheric, and the increasing number of upscale country houses also command high prices. B&Bs, *agriturismi* and private rentals offer the cheapest accommodation. In touristy areas you'll find a three-course dinner with wine will set you back €50-plus a head, but simple *trattorie* in more remote locations charge a fraction of that. Fuel costs are similar to those across Europe, but public transport remains comfortably inexpensive. State museums are generally discounted for EU citizens between 18-25 and for university students who usually pay half price (passport, ID or driving licence may be required).

Children

Children are usually made to feel welcome, and are readily accepted in restaurants. Although restaurants don't often have kids' menus, any restaurant will happily prepare a simple pasta with cheese or tomato sauce for the little ones. You can also ask for half portions. At the beach, children usually wear bathing suits and it is not customary to let them run around naked if they are over two years old. Babysitting services are available in many of the upper-range hotels. Children under the age of six are usually admitted to sights free of charge and those from six to 16 at 50 percent discount. Public transport is generally free for children under 1 metre.

Sicilian elder

Climate

April, May, June, September and October are the loveliest months, when Sicily enjoys a semblance of solitude combined with the pleasures of a mild climate. July and August, are crowded with Italian and foreign tourists and temperatures can get very hot indeed. If going to the beach is not your main concern, going in winter may also be an option: there's a lot to see and temperatures are mild with relatively frequent sunny days.

Clothing

Bring lightweight clothing and a hat during the hot summer months. In spring (April and May) and autumn (October and November) you will need a jacket or sweater for the evenings, though it can be warm in the sun. Winters, particularly in the mountainous central areas, can be cold. Mount Etna requires strong footwear in any season.

Crime and safety

Petty crime is the main problem for tourists: pickpocketing, bag-snatching and theft from cars, particularly in Palermo and Catania. Keep an eye on valuables at all times, and when driving always lock car doors and keep valuables hidden. If you are robbed, report it as soon as possible to the local police. You will need a copy of the declaration in order to claim on your insurance.

Kids in Santa Maria della Scala

Electricity

Sockets take two or three round-pronged plugs; supplies are 220-volts AC, 50 cycles. Visitors may require an adaptor, and those from North America will need a convertor as well.

Embassies and consulates

If your passport is lost or stolen you will need to obtain a police report and have proof of your identity to get a new one. Then contact your embassy in Rome (see below):

Australian Embassy: www.italy.embassy.gov.au

Canadian Embassy: www.canada.it (still works but the official link is

Caltagirone steps

Pastries are a Sicilian specialty

www.international.gc.ca/country-pays/splash/italy-italie.aspx?lang=eng)
Irish Embassy: www.dfa.ie/irish-embassy/italy
UK Embassy: www.gov.uk/world/organisations/british-embassy-rome
US Embassy: https://it.usembassy.gov

Emergencies

General emergences: 113; Police: 112; Fire: 115: Ambulance: 118; Breakdown/road assistance: 116

Etiquette

Dressing modestly in churches is expected for both males and females. Casual clothes are quite acceptable in most restaurants, but avoid swimwear except at beach establishments. If invited for dinner by locals, you are expected to always bring something: pastries, wine or flowers are always appreciated.

Green issues

A major problem has been illegal Mafia building with constructions on mountain slopes and protected coastal zones. But Sicilians generally are increasingly aware of their responsibilty for the environment. Nearly 9 percent of the land is now protected as nature reserves. Beautiful stretches of coastline and mountain regions are attracting cyclists and hikers, and the island has seen an increasing number of sustainable tourism projects created in recent years. Several specialist companies offer bike tours in rural Sicily and the islands, eg Sole&Bike (www.solebike.it). Many towns and resorts have bikes to rent and an increasing number of hotels offer free bikes to guests.

Health

Non-EU residents should have travel insurance to cover all eventualities. You will often be asked to pay for treatment up front, so keep all receipts for reimbursement. In many areas in summer there is a *Guardia Medica Turistica* (tourist emergency medical service) which functions 24 hours a day. Details are available

Fishing in Palermo

from pharmacies, tourist offices, hotels and local newspapers.

Pharmacies *(farmacie)* have green cross signs above the entrance; in each town, one stays open late and on Sundays on a rotating basis. The after-hour locations for the month are posted in all pharmacies. For serious cases or emergencies, dial 118 for an ambulance or head for the *Pronto Soccorso* (Accident and Emergency) of the local hospital.

Pharmacies and hospitals

A pharmacy *(farmacia)* is identified by a green cross. All main towns offer a 24-hour pharmacy service, with a night-time and Sunday rota. Duty pharmacists are posted on all pharmacy doors and published in the daily papers. For serious cases or emergencies, dial 118 for an ambulance or head for the *Pronto Soccorso* (Accident and Emergency) of the local hospital.

Internet facilities

Nearly all hotels and many cafes and restaurants and bars in Sicily offer WiFi to their clients. Except in remote rural areas, 3G, 4G and occasionally 5G coverage is pretty universal.

LGBTQ+ travellers

Attitudes are fairly relaxed in the main centres though rural areas tend to be more conservative. Taormina is still the focus for the native and foreign gay community. Its gay bars come and go. The gay scene also centres on Palermo and Catania which both host annual pride parades. Consult Arci-gay, the national gay rights organisation, www.arcigay.it, has branches in Palermo, Catania and Syracuse. To access bars and discos, you need to join the assoication, with a special membership card for foreigners.

Media

The main Italian papers (*Corriere della Sera* and *La Repubblica*) publish southern editions, but the local dailies are more popular. *Il Giornale di Sicilia*, Palermo's paper, covers western Sicily, and includes practical listings. *La Sicilia*, Catania's main paper, also has provincial supplements for Siracusa, Ragusa and Enna

Money

The unit of currency in Italy is the euro, written as €. Notes are denominated in 5, 10, 20, 50, 100 and 500; coins in 1 and 2 euros and 1, 2, 5, 10, 20 and 50 cents. Contactless payments are fast becoming the norm, though you should always have some cash handy. Although you can take euros out from cash machines directly from your home account, it is cheaper to load money onto an international digital account, such as Wise (www.wise.com) which can provide you with a digital or physical contactless card.

Lípari at dusk

Trápani dog

Tipping

A 10–15 percent service charge is usually included in restaurant bills, and although a tip will be appreciated, no extra is expected. For quick service in bars, leave a coin or two extra. Round up the fare for taxi drivers, and tip guides €5 per person.

Opening hours

Shops are generally open Mon–Sat 8am or 9am–1pm and 4–7.30pm but many non-food shops close on Monday and with the exception of supermarkets, food shops usually close on Wednesday. In Taormina and other major towns and resorts the shops are open daily.

Banks are open Mon–Fri 8.30am–1.30pm. Some also open for an hour or so in the afternoon.

Post offices are open weekdays from 8.20am–1.35pm, Saturdays from 8.20–12.35am. Major branches may stay open all day until 7pm, while in small places, local office may open only on selective days.

Many museums and monuments throughout Sicily have extended their opening hours, often seven days a week and into the early evening. Even so, hours vary widely. Smaller museums may open mornings only, or just for a couple of afternoons a week. Some are closed on Monday, and also Sunday afternoon. Most churches open early around 8am, close at noon, then open again for two to three hours at 4pm or 5pm. Don't be surprised to find churches or major sites closed for ongoing restoration. Local tourist boards can provide current opening times for sights in a particular town or region.

Police

There are three kinds of police in Italy: *vigili urbani*, who deal with petty crime, traffic, parking and other day-to-day matters; *carabinieri*, the highly trained national force who handle serious crime and civilian unrest, protect government figures and perform other high-profile tasks; and *polizia stradale*, who patrol the roadways. Any of these forces may answer a 113 emergency call, though the *carabinieri* have their own emergency number, 112.

Post

The postal service is notoriously slow. If you need to send an urgent letter, send it by Posta *Prioritaria*. Stamps *(francobolli)* are also available from tobacconists *(tabacchi)* and bars that also sell cigarettes.

Public holidays

Banks and most shops are closed on the following holidays:

1 January: New Year's Day
6 January: Epiphany
March/April: Easter Sunday and Monday
25 April: Liberation Day

Sampling the delights at this pasticceria in Erice

1 May: May Day
2 June: Republic Day
15 August: Ferragosto; Assumption Day
1 November: All Saints' Day
8 December: Feast of the Immaculate Conception
25 December: Christmas Day
26 December: Santo Stefano (Boxing Day)

Major holidays and festivals

New Year's Eve is very big business in Sicily: there is usually a large dinner followed by drinking, dancing and firecrackers. It falls in the middle of a long holiday period that begins on Christmas Eve and lasts until Epiphany on 6 January. The friendly witch *(befana)* who brings candy to the good kids and coal to the naughty ones is a strongly felt tradition in Italy and especially in Southern Italy. Easter is normally a three or four-day religious holiday, though businesses only close on Easter Sunday and Monday. Trápani is famous for its Easter procession, when 20 life-size wooden statues, dating from the 18th century, are paraded for 10 hours through the streets. The statues, or *Misteri*, are kept in the Chiesa del Purgatorio on Via Francesco d'Assisi (which unfortunately is usually closed).

Every city or town has its own patron Saint, celebrated with processions around the city centre, some of which end with suggestive ceremonies by the sea.

Feast of Saint Agata, Catania

Religion

Italy is a Catholic country. The hours of Mass vary, but each church has its own Mass timetable pinned on its main door.

Other denominations may practise their faith without hindrance and have their own services in Palermo and Catania.

Telephones

For calls within Italy, telephone numbers must be preceded by the full area code even if the call is made within the same district. When

Chiesa del Gesù, Palermo

View of Etna from a plane

phoning abroad form Italy dial 00, then the country code, followed by the city or area code and the number (omitting any initial 0). International dialling codes are 1 for the US and Canada, 44 for the UK, 353 for the Republic of Ireland, 61 for Australia, 64 for New Zealand. Hotels slap very large surcharges on long-distance calls.

Mobile (Cell) Phones

Check the international roaming rates with your provider prior to departure, and whether your phone can receive and make calls in Italy. Roaming rates are generally high for non-EU countries and if you are making a lot of calls or staying for some time it may be worth purchasing a SIM 'pay as you go' card available from many tobacconists as well as from the main providers (Wind, Tre, Tim).

Time zones

Italy and Sicily follow Central European Time (GMT+1) but, from the last Sunday in March to the last Sunday in October, the clocks advance one additional hour to become GMT+2. This means in summer when it is noon in Sicily it will be 11am in London and 6am in New York.

Toilets

Public toilets are hard to find, but you can usually use toilets in cafés and bars. In many cases the toilets are locked and you will have to ask for the key (chiave) at the till. Buying a drink at the same time will be appreciated. Major sites now have reasonable facilities.

Tourist information

Tourist offices are less common than they used to be, and funding problems means that those that have survived may be short staffed and have little material. Generally you can get good quality information online if you stick to reliable websites such as the ones below.

Websites

Useful sites are:
www.enit.it Italian government Tourist Board, covering all of Italy.

The port of Levanzo

'ww.visitsicily.info Official icilian tourist website.

'ww.parks.it Italian parks and eserves (then consult Sicily).

'ww.bestofsicily.com packed 'ith information on the sland; strong on culture.

'ww.visitpalermo.it All about Palermo.

'ww.thethinkingtraveller.com 'illas in Sicily, plus a useful and 1sightful guide to the island.

'rápani: Via Torrearsa 69, tel: 0923 31 701; www.apt.trapani.it

'ransport

∖rriving by air

icily currently has four international irports: Palermo (Falcone-Borsellino), Catania (Fontanarossa), 'rápani (Birgi) and Comiso (Pio a Torre). Travellers for Messina nd the Aeolian Islands could also onsider using Reggio di Calabria irport on the Italian mainland, ust across the Strait of Messina.

The islands of **Lampedusa** nd **Pantelleria** are linked by air ervices from Palermo or Trápani.

'alermo Airport

'alermo's Falcone-Borsellino airport www.gesap.it) is 30km (19 miles) vest of the capital at Punta Raisi. t is used by all the major airlines. The bus service Prestia e Comandè www.prestiaecomande.it) runs daily ervices from 5am 12.15am, every 30 minutes, linking the airport with Palermo's Terminal Stazione Centrale (Central Station) with seven stops in Palermo en route. Tickets can be purchased online or at the ticket office in the Arrivals Hall. A taxi from the airport to downtown Palermo costs €50–60.

Catania Airport

Catania's Fontanarossa airport (www.aeroporto.catania.it) is 5km (3 miles) south of the city. There is an Alibus service departing every 20 minutes from 5am to midnight for Stazione Centrale (the central railway station), taking 20 minutes. Tickets can be bought on the bus. Other bus services link the airport to Siracusa, Ragusa, Noto, Taormina and many other cities in eastern Sicily, as well as Palermo.

Comiso Airport (Ragusa)

The Aeroporto di Comiso Pio La Torre (also known as Vincenzo Magliocco) is used by low-cost carriers and Alitalia. AST buses connect the airport with Ragusa while several other bus companies link it with Agrigento, Módica and Catania.

Trápani Airport

Trápani-Birgi's Vincenzo Florio airport (www.airgest.it), used by low-cost carriers, is 15km (9 miles) southeast of Trápani. AST buses (www.aziendasicilianatrasporti.it) link the airport to Trápani roughly every hour, taking 45 minutes, from where you can pick up connections to Palermo, Agrigento and Marsala.

iew to the Egadi Islands

Arriving by rail

The Italian mainland is linked to Sicily by train, with Milan, Rome and Naples the best connecting stations to the south. Unfortunately, the great improvements in the Italian rail system do not extend to Sicily. Trains are operated by Italian State Railways (www.trenitalia.com). All trains from Italy to Sicily cross from Villa San Giovanni on the Italian mainland via ferry across the Strait of Messina to Messina's port.

Arriving by sea

Ferries link Sicily with Naples, Genova (Genoa) and Salerno with Cagliari in Sardinia; there are also links with Tunis and Malta. Hydrofoils *(aliscafi)* operate between Sicily and its smaller islands (see under Transport within Sicily below). Sicily can be combined with Malta on a two-island holiday using Virtu Ferries (www.virtuferries.com) from the southern port of Pozzallo.

Ferry tickets can be booked online (though there is no need for the Messina/Villa San Giovanni crossing). The main operators are SNAV (www.snav.it), Grandi Navi Veloci (www.gnv.it), Tirrenia (www.tirrenia.it) and Grimaldi Lines (www.grimaldi-lines.com). There are cabins on the longer routes, and these must be booked well in advance for high summer. Remember that sailing schedules are prone to change, especially in winter months when the seas can turn rough.

Arriving by car

Driving to Sicily from the UK takes at least 24 hours – realistically count on at least five days. To bring a car into Italy you will need a current driving licence and valid insurance. You must carry your driving licence, car registration, insurance documents and passport with you at all times when driving. You are also required to carry a triangular warning sign and a high visibility vest.

Transport around Sicily

Driving

A car in Sicily is a great help exploring the island, though in cities it can be easier and less nerve-racking to use public transport or taxis. The network of roads has much improved, though you can still expect potholes even on some of the major roads. A system of mainly toll-free motorways *(autostrade)* crosses parts of the island, linking the main cities. Elsewhere roads can be quite slow-going, especially in the mountainous regions.

The main frustrations of driving in Sicily are parking (see below), negotiating town centres (which often have complex one-way systems and poor signing to the centre) and darting motorbike and scooter riders)who drive too fast and frequently recklessly.

Car hire

Major hire companies include Avis, Europcar, Hertz and Sixt. You'll

Foro Italico, Palermo

nd offices in the main airports, but 's usually cheaper to book ahead hrough major travel websites.

Drivers must present their own ational driving licence. Credit-ard imprints are taken as a deposit nd are usually the only form of ayment acceptable. 'Inclusive' prices o not generally include personal ccident insurance or insurance gainst damage to windscreens, yres and wheels. Pay attention o your return time – it's easy to et charged for an extra day.

ules and regulations

)rive on the right, pass on the left. peed limits are 50km/h (30mph) n towns and built-up areas, 90km/h 55mph) on main roads and 130km/h 80mph) on motorways. Speeding nd other traffic offences are subject o heavy on-the-spot fines.

The use of hand-held mobiles vhile driving is prohibited. The blood lcohol limit is 0.05 percent, and olice occasionally make random reath tests. Seat belts are compulsory n the front and back. Lights must e used on all out-of-town roads.

'arking

'inding a parking space in town entres is notoriously tricky. Historic entres are often inaccessible to cars, ther than those of residents, though isitors staying at hotels with parking acilities are allowed access. Look for white 'P' on a blue background or parking lots and garages at the fringes of the town centre. Illegal parking valets *(parcheggiatori abusive)* are very common in the big centres and on the coast in high season, and will ask you for a euro or two to 'protect' your car, often without helping you park at all. If you don't pay, expect to return amnd find your car has some minor damage.

On the autostrada towards Noto

Fuel

Petrol *(benzina)* is readily available, and there are many 24-hour stations with self-service dispensers that accept euro notes and credit cards, though it's wise to always bring cash in case the credit card machine is out of order. Electric car charging points are slowly becoming more common.

asy-going Sicilians

The train line at Taormina

Rail

Trains are operated by Italian State Railways, Ferrovie dello Stato (www.trenitalia.com). The rail system in Sicily is cheap but slow, and not really convenient for seeing all of the island. The east of the island is better linked than the west. Messina is well linked to both Palermo and Catania. Catania is linked with the major cities (though trains take far longer from here to Palermo than the coach) and is the starting point of the Ferrovia Circumetnea, the narrow-gauge train that calls at all villages around Mount Etna on a circular route (see page 87).

Seat reservations are obligatory on the faster Intercity services. Tickets for all trains must be stamped in the yellow machines on the platforms before boarding the train. Failure to do so can incur a hefty on-the-spot fine.

Taxi

In cities, taxis are best telephoned or found at taxi ranks in the main squares of the larger towns. Licensed taxis are white, with a Taxi sign on the roof, and have a meter which should be turned on at the start of the journey. When it comes to tipping, it's usual to round up the fare. Beware of touts without meters who may approach you at airports and large train stations.

Coach and bus

Fast bus services, operated by many different companies, link Sicily's main towns and offer relatively speedy access to the interior and the south. Generally speaking, coaches are more reliable and quicker than trains, but they cost more.

City buses have a flat fare and tickets are valid for 75 minutes, including change of bus routes. Bus tickets, available from bars, tobacconists, and from machines at bus terminals and metro stations, must be validated in the machine on the bus.

Ferries/hydrofoils

Getting to the Aeolian Islands. Access by ferry and hydrofoil to the islands is shortest and most frequent

Sicilian local beating the heat

rom Milazzo (near Messina) on the orth coast, accessed by autostrada rom Palermo or Messina, or by rain from both cities (although note hat the train station is on the edge f town, and if there is no bus, a axi will cost €15). In the summer, here are up to 11 hydrofoils a day o Lípari and Vulcano, and six a day o Salina. In high season there is lso a limited service to the islands rom Palermo. Hydrofoils are faster nd more expensive, but ferries give ou better views. Hydrofoil services, un by Liberty Lines (www.liberty ines.it) are more likely to be ancelled than ferries in bad weather. Ferries are mainly run by Caronte Tourist (www.carontetourist. t) and NGI (www.ngi-spa.it). **Getting to the Egadi Islands.** Ferries operated by Siremar (www.siremar. t) and hydrofoils by Liberty Lines (www.libertylines.it), run from Trápani several times a day in season o the Egadi Islands (Favignana, Lévanzo and Maréttimo).

Visas and passports

Visas are not required by visitors from the UK EU countries. A current passport or valid Identification Card is sufficient. For visitors from the US, Canada, Australia or New Zealand a visa is not required, but a valid passport is essential for entry to be granted for a stay of up to three months. Nationals of most other countries require a visa. This must be obtained in advance from an Italian Embassy or Consulate.

Wine resort tours

Sicily has seen an increasing number of appealing wine estates where visitors can usually also spend the night, dine or do a cookery or wine-tasting course. Just outside Alcamo, the Sirignano Wine Resort is a delightful organic estate run by the family of the Marchsi de Gregorio (www.sirignanowineresort.it). Guests stay in converted farmworkers' cottages and sample the superb wines over meals cooked by an outstanding chef. For more comprehensive guided tours through Sicily's wine tradition, visitors can contact a number of wine tour companies: Wine Tours in Sicily (www.winetourinsicily.com) is one of the most popular.

Women

Women travellers will invariably come across Sicilians with a roving eye, but serious harassment and sexual assaults are rare. Use common sense and beware of bag-snatchers and pickpockets. In some of the smaller internal towns it is unusual to see women sitting at a bar alone, and that may attract attention. After dark it is wise to avoid the unlit backstreets in Palermo and Catania. The resorts of Taormina and Cefalù are normally safe.

Catania market

Language

Italian is relatively easy to pick up, if you have any knowledge of French or Spanish (or a grounding in Latin). Most hotels have staff who speak some English, and unless you go well off the beaten track, you should have little problem communicating in shops or restaurants. However, there are places not on the tourist circuit where you will have the chance to practise your Italian, and local people will think more of you for making an effort. Here are a few basics to help you get started.

Useful phrases

General

Yes *Sì*
No *No*
Thank you *Grazie*
Many thanks *Mille grazie/Tante grazie*
You're welcome *Prego*
All right/That's fine *Va bene*
Please *Per favore/Per cortesia*
Excuse me (to get attention) *Scusi*
Excuse me (in a crowd) *Permesso*
Could you help me? (formal) *Potrebbe aiutarmi?*
Certainly *Ma certo/Certamente*
Can you show me…? *Può indicarmi…?*
Can you help me, please? *Può aiutarmi, per cortesia?*
I need… *Ho bisogno di…*
I'm lost *Mi sono perso*
I'm sorry *Mi dispiace*
I don't know *Non lo so*
I don't understand *Non capisco*
Do you speak English/French/Spanish? *Parla inglese/francese/spagnolo?*
Could you speak more slowly? *Può parlare più lentamente, per favore?*
Could you repeat that please? *Può ripetere, per piacere?*
How much does it cost? *quanto costa?*
this one/that one *questo/quello*
Have you got…? *Avete…?*

At a bar/restaurant

I'd like to book a table *Vorrei prenotare un tavolo*
Have you got a table for… *Avete un tavolo per…*
I have a reservation *Ho prenotato*
lunch *il pranzo*
supper *la cena*
I'm a vegetarian/vegan *Sono vegetariano/a* vegano/a
May we have the menu? *Ci dia la carta?*
What would you like? *Che cosa prende?*
I'd like… *Vorrei…*
mineral water *acqua minerale*
fizzy/still *gasata/naturale*
a bottle of *una bottiglia di*
a glass of *un bicchieri di*

Sicilians love to chat

ed wine *vino rosso*
vhite wine *vino bianco*
eer *una birra*

Jumbers

Jne *uno*
Two *due*
Three *tre*
Four *quattro*
Five *cinque*
Six *sei*
Seven *sette*
Eight *otto*
Nine *nove*
Ten *dieci*
Twenty *venti*
Thirty *trenta*
Forty *quaranta*
Fifty *cinquanta*
One hundred *cento*
One thousand *mille*

Getting around

What time do you open/ close? *A che ora apre/chiude?*
Closed for the holidays *Chiuso per ferie*
Where can I buy tickets? *Dove posso fare i biglietti?*
What time does the train leave? *A che ora parte il treno?*
Can you tell me where to get off? *Mi può dire dove devo scendere?*
Where is the nearest bank/hotel? *Dov'è la banca/l'albergo più vicino?*
On the right *a destra*
On the left *a sinistra*
Go straight on *Va sempre diritto*

Lipari excursion shop

Online

What is the WiFi password? *Qual è la password Wi-Fi?*
Is the WiFi free? *Il WiFi è gratis?*
How do I turn the computer on/off? *Come si accende/spegne il computer?*
Can I...? *Posso...?*
access the internet *collegarmi (a Internet)*
check e-mail *controllare le e-mail*
print *stampare*
plug in/charge my laptop/ iPhone/iPad? *collegare/ricaricare il mio portatile/iPhone/iPad?*
log on/log off *si fa il login/logout*
What's your e-mail? *Qual è la sua e-mail?*
My e-mail is... *La mia e-mail è...*

Souvenirs for sale

Books and film

With its rural areas, its beauty and its history, Sicily has inspired many authors and film directors. The Mafia, with its mysteries and crime stories, has also had an important role in literature and cinema, giving Sicily a type of fame the Sicilians would have been happier without.

Books

History and culture

The Leopard, by Giuseppe Tomasi di Lampedusa. This is both the classic Sicilian novel and one of the most important novels in Italian literature.
The Last Leopard: A Life of Giuseppe Tomasi di Lampedusa, by David Gilmour. This is a sensitive literary biography and companion to *The Leopard* itself, based on interviews with the author's adopted son and full access to the family archives.
The Normans in Sicily, by John Julius Norwich. This remains the best introduction to the "other" Norman Conquest, including of Southern Italy and Sicily – led by the great Euro-adventurers.
Cavalleria Rusticana and Other Stories, I Malavoglia, History of a Capinera, by Giovanni Verga. One of Italy's most important authors, Verga was a realist writer best known for his depictions of rural Sicily and poverty. His most famous novel is *Cavalleria Rusticana.*
Fredrick II: A Medieval Emperor, by David Abulafia. A biography of Fredrick II.

Crime and society

The Shape of Water, The Terracotta Dog, The Voice of the Violin and ***The Snack Thief***, by Andrea Camilleri. These detective stories/ thrillers are worldwide best-sellers, helped by the Montalbano films.
Boss of Bosses, by Clare Longrigg. This account covers the role and importance of Bernardo Provenzano, the Mafia boss *(capo di tutti capi)* who was arrested in 2006 in Corleone and died in jail in 2016.
The Day of the Owl, by Leonardo Sciascia. This novel about the Mafia was written by a rigorous writer and politician (1921–83) often known as 'the conscience of Sicily'.
Midnight in Sicily, by Peter Robb. Personal insights and trenchant observations on Sicilian society, customs, relationships, art, food, history and the Mafia.
No Questions Asked, by Clare Longrigg. This account covers the varied role of women in the Cosa Nostra, whom the author persuaded to talk.

Taormina's Teatro Greco

Travel and general

Bagheria, by Dacia Maraini. The author, the daughter of a Sicilian princess, revisits the family's ancestral villa in Bagheria, in an attempt to come to terms with her past and with the desecration of this once glorious town.

Bitter Almonds, by Mary Taylor Simeti and Maria Grammatico. This foodie memoir is inspired by a disappearing Sicily, linked to the convents producing pastries, notably the almond pastries in Erice.

Children of the Volcano by Ros Belford. Inspiring and humorous memoir charting the excitement and challenges of an English mother and her children living on the Aeolian island of Salina.

Clay Ghosts in Sicily, by Angie Voluti. Set in post-war Palermo, this quirky new novel features a lovelorn young Sicilian sculptress haunted by memories conjured up by visits to the capital, with its secret tunnels and dilapidated palaces.

Good Girls Don't Wear Trousers, by Lara Cardella. Living in a stifling Sicilian town in the early 1960s, teenage Annetta dreams that wearing trousers will give her freedom.

A House in Sicily, by Daphne Phelps An affectionate travel memoir centred on Casa Cuseni, a Taormina pensione that welcomed artists and writers such as Tennessee Williams and Roald Dahl.

Made in Sicily, Giorgio Locatelli. This new gastronomic tour of Sicily presents the celebrity chef's simplest yet most authentic island recipes.

Films

Cabiria (1914). A silent film set in ancient Sicily during the Punic Wars.

Cinema Paradiso (1988). Flashbacks of the protagonist's childhood give a glimpse of Sicily in the 1950s to the soundtrack of Ennio Morricone.

Divorce, Italian Style (*Divorzio all'italiana*; 1961). This comedy by Pietro Germi portrays passion and romantic relationships in 1960s Sicily.

The Postman (*Il Postino*; 1994). The story of an exiled poet who lives in Lampedusa, and of his friendship with his postman (Massimo Troisi) who learns to love poetry.

The Star Maker (*L'Uomo delle Stelle*; 1995). This film by Giuseppe Tornatore tells the story of a fake movie director who travels rural Sicily, offering to shoot screen test of aspiring actors.

The Leopard (*Il Gattopardo*; 1968). Luchino Visconti's take on Tomasi de Lampedusa's famous novel.

Stromboli (1949). This movie by Roberto Rossellini depicts the culture and mentality of the inhabitants of Stromboli from the eyes of a displaced Lithuanian woman who moves there after the war.

The Godfather (1972). Francis Ford Coppola's American crime story tells the story of the fictional Corleone Mafia family.

Johnny Stecchino (1991). An entertaining comedy in which bus driver Dante (Roberto Benigni) is mistaken for a fierce Mafia gangster.

Romantic Ortigia

Bar Vitelli from The Godfather

About this book

The Rough Guides Walks & Tours series helps you discover the world's most exciting destinations through our expert-curated trip plans: a range of walks and tours designed to suit all budgets, interests and trip lengths. These walks, driving tours and site excursions cover the destination's most quintessential attractions as well as a range of lesser-known sights, while food and drink stops for refreshments en route are highlighted in boxes. If you're not sure which walk to pick, our Best walks & tours for... feature suggests which ones work best for particular interests. The introduction provides a destination overview, while the directory supports the walks and tours with all the essential information you need, as well as our pick of where to stay while you are there and select restaurant listings, to complement the more low-key options given in the trip plans.

About the authors

Rough Guides Walks & Tours Sicily was updated by Ros Belford who co-authored the first edition of the Rough Guide to Italy, and has since written and broadcasted extensively about Italy and the Mediterranean. She lives in Cambridge and spends as much time as she can in Siracusa and on the Aeolian island of Salina.

Her work builds on original content by Susie Boulton, Lisa Gerard-Sharp and Daniel Mosseri.

Help us update

We've gone to a lot of effort to ensure that this edition of the **Rough Guides Walks & Tours Sicily** is accurate and up-to-date. However, things change – places get "discovered", new gems open up, restaurants and rooms raise prices or lower standards. If you feel we've got it wrong or left something out, we'd like to know, and if you can remember the address, the website, whether or not it was free to enter – so much the better.

Please send your comments with the subject line "**Rough Guides Walks & Tours Sicily Update**" to mail@roughguides.com. We'll acknowledge all contributions and send a copy of the next edition (or any other Rough Guide if you prefer) for the very best emails.

Credits

Rough Guides Walks & Tours Sicily
Editor: Beth Williams
Author: Ros Belford
Picture Editor: Piotr Kala
Picture Manager: Tom Smyth
Cartography: Katie Bennett
Layout: Grzegorz Madejak
Production Operations Manager: Katie Bennett
Publishing Technology Manager: Rebeka Davies
Head of Publishing: Sarah Clark
Photo credits: Belmond Grand Hotel Timeo 109; Belmond Villa Sant'Andrea 103; Bigstock 12, 29, 87, 91R, 92; Caol Ishka 106; Dreamstime 17R, 18/19, 58/59, 64, 77R, 96/97, 97R, 114, 118, 119R; Fotolia 54, 69; Hotel Signum 107, 110; iStock 7M, 8/9, 20, 63R, 103R, 105R, 111, 115, 118/119, 135; Kempinski Giardino di Costanza 104, 105; La Madia 116/117; Neil Buchan-Grant/Apa Publications 4BL, 4MR, 6MC, 6BC, 7T, 7MR, 7MR, 10, 11R, 10/11, 13R, 14, 15R, 16, 16/17, 21R, 20/21, 22, 22/23, 23R, 25, 26, 26/27, 27R, 28, 33, 36, 37, 38, 38/39, 40, 41, 42, 42/43, 44, 45, 46, 46/47, 48, 48/49, 49R, 50, 51, 52, 53R, 52/53, 55, 56, 57R, 56/57, 60/61, 62, 62/63, 65, 66, 66/67, 67R, 68, 70/71, 72, 72/73, 73R, 74, 75R, 74/75, 76, 76/77, 78, 78/79, 79R, 80, 81R, 80/81, 83, 84, 84/85, 86, 88, 89R, 88/89, 90, 90/91, 93, 95, 96, 108/109, 120/121, 122, 124, 124/125, 125R, 126, 127, 129, 130, 131, 132, 133, 134, 136, 136/137; Shutterstock 1, 4T, 4BR, 6TL, 6ML, 12/13, 14/15, 24, 30/31, 32, 34, 35, 39R, 43R, 47R, 70, 71R, 82, 85R, 94, 98/99, 100, 101, 102, 108R, 112, 113, 116, 117R, 123, 128, 137R
Cover credits: Nice pots, Cefalu **iStock**

Printed by Elma Basim in Turkey

This book was produced using **Typefi** automated publishing software.

A catalogue record for this book is available from the British Library.

First Edition 2025

ISBN: 9781835292341

Distribution

UK, Ireland and Europe
Apa Publications (UK) Ltd
mail@roughguides.com
United States and Canada
Two Rivers
ips@ingramcontent.com
Australia and New Zealand
Woodslane
info@woodslane.com.au
Worldwide
Apa Publications (UK) Ltd
mail@roughguides.com

Special Sales, Content Licensing and CoPublishing

Rough Guides can be purchased in bulk quantities at discounted prices. We can create special editions, personalized jackets and corporate imprints tailored to your needs.
mail@roughguides.com
http://roughguides.com

EU Representative

LOGOS EUROPE, 9 rue Nicolas Poussin, 17000, LA ROCHELLE, France
Contact@logoseurope.eu; +33 (0) 667937378

Index

O

P

R

MAP LEGEND

Start of tour
Tour & route direction
Recommended sight
Recommended restaurant/café

Place of interest
Tourist information
Statue/monument
Ancient site

Cable car
Villa, refuge
Cave